WILLIAMSBURG BRAY SCHOOL

A History Through Records, Reflections, and Rediscovery

EDITED BY MAUREEN ELGERSMAN LEE
AND NICOLE BROWN

THE COLONIAL WILLIAMSBURG FOUNDATION
WILLIAMSBURG, VIRGINIA

WILLIAM & MARY BRAY SCHOOL LAB
WILLIAMSBURG, VIRGINIA

© 2024 by The Colonial Williamsburg Foundation
All rights reserved. Published 2024.

35 34 33 32 31 30 29 28 27 26 25 24   1 2 3 4 5 6 7

Designed by Katie Roy

LCCN 2024945582

ISBN 978-0-87935-303-2

Colonial Williamsburg is a registered trade name of The Colonial Williamsburg Foundation, a not-for-profit educational institution.

The Colonial Williamsburg Foundation
PO Box 1776
Williamsburg, VA 23187
colonialwilliamsburg.org

William & Mary
PO Box 8795
Williamsburg, VA 23187
www.wm.edu/sites/brayschool/

Printed in Canada

Image credits: cover (student list), 26, 64, 92, 114, 136, Bodleian Library, University of Oxford [2024]; 12, Plan de la ville et environs de Williamsburg en Virginie (Frenchman's Map of Williamsburg, Virginia), 1782, Special Collections Research Center, William & Mary Libraries; 40, John Waring to Rev. Dawson, February 29, 1760, Tracy W. McGregor Library of American History, Albert and Shirley Small Special Collections Library, University of Virginia.

To the Williamsburg Bray School Scholars—those named, those whose names we are yet to discover, and those whose names we may never know.

Contents

INTRODUCTION

PRESIDENT CLIFF FLEET, THE COLONIAL WILLIAMSBURG FOUNDATION
PRESIDENT KATHERINE ROWE, WILLIAM & MARY
A Partnership — *9*

TERRY L. MEYERS
A Connection — *13*

MATTHEW WEBSTER
A Discovery — *17*

ANTONIO T. BLY
One Scholar's Story: Isaac's Homecoming — *23*

MAUREEN ELGERSMAN LEE AND NICOLE BROWN
Legacies of the Williamsburg Bray School — *27*

Founders of the Williamsburg Bray School:
The Associates of Dr. Bray — *30*

The Williamsburg Bray School, 1760–1774: A Brief History — *32*

Williamsburg Bray School Chronology — *36*

Bray School Student Residence Map — *38*

Records and Reflections — *41*

ONE / ESTABLISHING THE WILLIAMSBURG BRAY SCHOOL, 1760–1761 — *43*

JULIE RICHTER
Preparing to Open the Bray School on September 29, 1760 — *50*

JASON A. CHEN
Tensions in Expanding the Reach of Education:
Reflections on the Past and Present — *53*

FALLON BURNER
Colonialism & Education: Comparing the Brafferton
Indian School and the Williamsburg Bray School   56

JOHN C. VAN HORNE
Revisiting the Williamsburg Bray School after Fifty Years   59

ROBERT "BOBBY" A. BRAXTON
The Tentacles of the Williamsburg Bray School   62

TWO / 1762: EXCEEDING EXPECTATIONS   67

JANICE CANADAY
Remembering London   79

JOHNETTE GORDON-WEAVER
The Talented Tenth of Their Generation   82

TONIA CANSLER MERIDETH
By Which They Might Be Distinguished   85

LESLIE GASTON-BIRD
Rediscovering Roots and Rethinking Education   88

ADAM CANADAY
The Legacy We Carry   91

THREE / 1765: PATTERNS OF GROWTH AND ATTRITION   95

HOPE WRIGHT
Clara, Johanna, Hannah, and Me   100

CRYSTAL HASKINS
Your Words Are Your Wand   103

BURNELL IRBY
The Williamsburg Bray School: Conflict and Community   106

DEVIN CANADAY
Exposure to Knowledge Is a Gateway to New Possibilities   109

VICKI ANDERSON SIMONS
Unfinished Business: The Williamsburg Bray School Experiment   112

FOUR / 1769: AN INCREASINGLY FRACTURED
RELATIONSHIP   117

THEODORA "TEDDI" ASHBY
A Bray School Descendant   123

JODY LYNN ALLEN
A Tale of Two Points of View … *126*

YVONNE L. "BONNIE" JOHNSON
Asking Hard Questions … *129*

JANISE PARKER
Progress: What Did It Mean for the Williamsburg
Bray School Scholar? … *132*

JACQUELINE BRIDGEFORTH-WILLIAMS
The Legacy That Haunts: Our Continued Struggle for
Racial Justice in Education … *135*

FIVE / **ENDINGS AND BEGINNINGS, 1774-1777** … *139*

CECILIA WEAVER
Robert Carter Nicholas on the Williamsburg Bray School:
An Intersection of Religion and Economy … *145*

RACHEL HOGUE
Personhood in Place of Silence: Reflecting on the Absence
of Bray School Scholars in Robert Carter Nicholas's 1774 Letter … *148*

DAWN EDMISTON
Closing the Williamsburg Bray School … *151*

JAJUAN S. JOHNSON
Where Have We Been? The Williamsburg Bray School's
Closure, Freedom Making, and the Black Educational Tradition … *154*

ASHLEY McCUISTION
A Legacy of Learning: Archaeology at the Williamsburg
Bray School Site … *157*

ANN MARIE STOCK, PRESIDENTIAL LIAISON FOR STRATEGIC CULTURAL
PARTNERSHIPS, WILLIAM & MARY
Afterword … *160*

ELIZABETH DREMBUS
Linking the Present with the Past
A Genealogy Supplement … *163*

Acknowledgments … *166*

Bibliography/For Further Reading … *168*

A Partnership

By Cliff Fleet and Katherine Rowe

An unassuming white building had long stood tucked away on Prince George Street behind the sorority houses at William & Mary. Used as a dormitory for women and then a storage building for the Department of Military Science's Reserve Officer Training Corps (ROTC) program, its story had been lost to time.

And what an incredible story it tells. Long hidden in plain sight, we now know it to be the original Williamsburg Bray School, America's oldest surviving school for Black children, enslaved and free. Its historic rediscovery in 2020 is the result of a unique partnership between our institutions—the world's largest U.S. history museum and the nation's first university—and a community of descendants who trace their ancestry to the students who came and learned at the school during the eighteenth century. Today, the Bray School is redefining how we understand the complicated, intersecting roles of faith, race, and education at the time of America's founding.

The search for the Williamsburg Bray School began with the work of Terry Meyers, a William & Mary English professor who was diligently exploring hidden histories of our local community. As Virginia's colonial capital at the time of the American Revolution, Williamsburg had played a critical role in the formation of our democratic republic. By uncovering the community's forgotten and long-ignored histories, Dr. Meyers was expanding our nation's understanding of its origin story.

For years he had puzzled over an intriguing question: Could this humble structure, home to generations of undergraduates, be the Williamsburg Bray School? The research remained inconclusive, so in 2020 we decided to answer the question once and for all—by taking the building apart.

As soon as we removed the first piece of wood siding, we knew we had found an eighteenth-century building. Research soon revealed that the logs used in the construction of the structure were cut in the fall of 1759 and the spring of 1760. This information, in combination with other research findings, left no doubt that we had found the original school structure. It was a stunning revelation that we knew held deep implications for our understanding of colonial-era Williamsburg.

Exciting as it was, the discovery quickly led to another series of complicated questions. What should we do with this important information and the historic building itself? How might such a finding increase our understanding of our nation's origins? How might we broadly disseminate the stories it reveals?

We continued moving forward as partners, leveraging both our institutions' resources and expertise. With support from the Descendant Community, we decided to move this delicate structure to The Colonial Williamsburg Foundation's Historic Area, where its world-renowned preservationists, craftsmen, and craftswomen could meticulously research and reconstruct the building itself. William & Mary, home to the nation's preeminent early American history program, would launch the Bray School Lab on Colonial Williamsburg's grounds, where scholars would collaborate with Descendant Community members to research the school's students and its impact on the wider community on the cusp of revolution. With these findings and the lessons learned from restoring the building itself, Colonial Williamsburg would create new public programming designed to educate Americans about our shared history.

Today we approach the 250th anniversary of the school's closing in 2024, and the U.S. Semiquincentennial in 2026. We are committed to ensuring that the origin stories of our nation become every American's shared story: a bridge to unite us across our divides. In sharing this history with the world, we must continue exploring not only its triumphs, but also its tragedies—for only in doing so can we better understand and address the challenges we face today. The insights gleaned from the Williamsburg Bray School are by turns triumphant, unsettling, tragic, and hopeful. In their fullness, they offer a critical opportunity for all of us: to better understand the formation of our democratic republic, to trace the complicated evolution of our society, and to move forward together.

The city of Williamsburg has already witnessed the power of this project. When we moved the building on February 10, 2023, in a slow and careful trip from William & Mary's campus to its new home in Colonial Williamsburg's Historic Area, thousands filled the sidewalks to be part of the historic event. Visitors gathered from nearby neighborhoods and across the world.

One small group showed us history at its best. As the building progressed towards its new site, children from the local elementary school lined the street. They held signs with the names of Black students known to have studied at the Bray School. Powerfully linking the present with the past, the children of 2023 welcomed these long-forgotten scholars from the 1760s into the Bray School of today. Here, we will continue to remember and affirm their contributions to our country.

Cliff Fleet is president and CEO of The Colonial Williamsburg Foundation, the world's largest U.S. history museum.

Katherine Rowe is president of William & Mary, the nation's first university, founded in 1693.

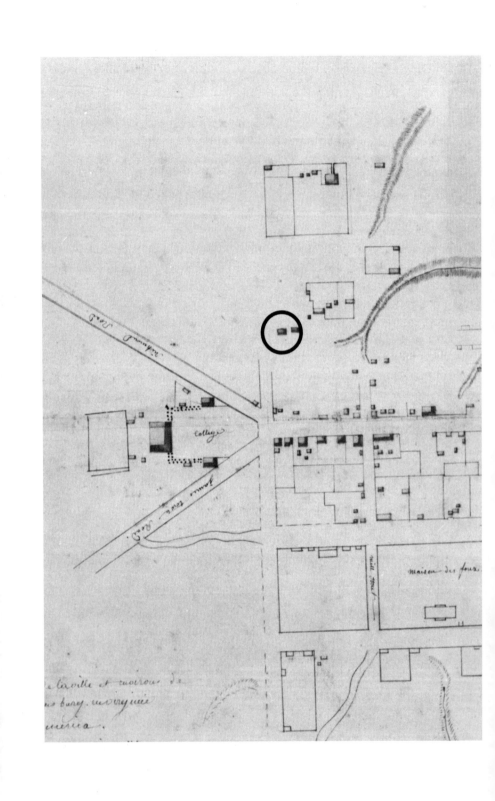

A Connection

By Terry L. Meyers

February 10, 2023: Charter Day at William & Mary. As I approach being eighty years old, I watch part of my legacy, the Bray-Digges House, being eased away from its site on the William & Mary campus for the last ninety-three years. A connection to the university is broken. But two others remain, in the founding of the school and in the story of my discovering the original structure.

The first connection. When Benjamin Franklin came to Williamsburg in 1756 on Post Office business, the president and faculty of the college took the opportunity to award him William & Mary's first honorary degree. In London four years later, Franklin became a member of an English evangelical philanthropy, the Associates of Dr. Bray. The Associates asked him to identify the best next places to site their schools for the religious education of Black children, enslaved and free.

Williamsburg was on his short list.

Enmeshed as Virginia was in the cruelty of chattel slavery, Williamsburg might have seemed a chancy location. But educating Black children in "the Principles of Christianity," a Christianity that preached subservience within a rigid class and racial hierarchy, had a pragmatic as well as a spiritual goal: "by making them good Christians they would necessarily become better Servants."

Many enslavers were skeptical, of course, believing it dangerous to educate Black children and thereby plant the seeds of insolence and rebellion. But Franklin had found in William & Mary a school whose president and clerical faculty were already instructing Black Virginians in the tenets of the Anglican Church and even contemplating founding a school for that. Franklin recommended President Thomas Dawson, once rector of Bruton Parish, to be a trustee of the Bray School alongside William Hunter, printer for the Virginia colony.

William & Mary was a powerful institution. It supported the Bray School and, as part of the colonial power structure, it could (and did) help protect the school from its many skeptics. Of all the Bray schools in the colonies, Williamsburg's was one of the most enduring, operating from 1760 to 1774.

The second William & Mary connection is the one with me, a William & Mary professor of English.

How did a specialist in Victorian poetry come to rediscover a forgotten eighteenth-century structure on campus? Well, one thing I noticed when we moved here in 1970 was that my century, the nineteenth century, had been erased.

It is hard to live in Williamsburg and not become interested in its history. I did. But I became interested in that missing century, the years between 1780 and 1924, between colonial Williamsburg and Colonial Williamsburg. I kept my eyes open for nineteenth-century Williamsburg, including local accounts such as one that proved central.

In 2002, longtime resident Ed Belvin published some reminiscences, *Williamsburg Facts and Fiction: 1900–1950*. The book is rich in local lore. I was especially intrigued when Belvin mentioned a building he said had belonged to Dudley Digges. He had the wrong Digges in mind, but he was clearly dating the structure to the eighteenth century. It was, he said, moved from its original site "across the street where it is still used by the College in a greatly altered state."

That baffled me.

I consulted Louise Kale, then executive director of the Historic Campus. She knew nothing of an eighteenth-century building on campus beyond the famous ones. Louise and I each explored the campus "across the street" from the first site of the Digges House, at the corner of Boundary and Prince George streets. Neither of us could see anything resembling an eighteenth-century house.

I just about gave up, thinking that any building moved to campus so long ago had surely been demolished.

But I had one more thought: I should visit Colonial Williamsburg's Rockefeller Library.

That did it. I was handed a file that had pictures of the house and more. "Greatly altered" was an understatement, but when I went back and saw the house at 524 Prince George Street, which Louise had thought might be the prize, I could mentally remove the additions and adjust the roof line. An eighteenth-century tenement building appeared. The chimneys were a clue; though embedded in additions, they originally were exterior.

The file included newspaper clippings. The house had been well known in the 1930s and 1940s—though no one suspected that it had housed a school. Knowledge of it had faded. Ed Chappell, a Colonial Williamsburg architectural historian, did later tell me his predecessor had told him it was an eighteenth-century structure. Archival work showed it had even been offered to the restoration in 1930 as, wrongly, one of the oldest houses in Williamsburg—seemingly confused for another house built decades earlier.

From that point my research proceeded, with help from many, and finally appeared in the June 19, 2004, edition of the *Virginia Gazette*.

The timing was good. The structure, I was told, had been slated to be demolished soon.

Terry L. Meyers, PhD, retired from William & Mary as Chancellor Professor, Emeritus, of English after 46 years of teaching. He was active with the Williamsburg Historical Records Association, which he served as president, and he was involved with the development of The Lemon Project at William & Mary.

A Discovery

By Matthew Webster

I remember exactly when we knew we had found the Williamsburg Bray School. It was 8:06 p.m. on Saturday, June 20, 2020. Several months before, we had been asked to look at the building to see whether we could conclusively identify it as the Bray School. I had crawled under the building in the heart of William & Mary's campus, looking for evidence that would help date the structure.

The building, which then housed the university's Department of Military Science, was called the Prince George Street House. Also known as the Digges House, it had been moved to Prince George Street in 1930 to make way for the construction of the Brown Hall dormitory. Terry Meyers, now Chancellor Professor of English, Emeritus, at William & Mary, suggested that this building had been depicted on the 1782 *Frenchman's Map*—a document likely drawn by a member of Rochambeau's army following the 1781 battle at Yorktown, and used as a billeting map for housing the French troops. Meyers suspected that this was actually the building that housed the Williamsburg Bray School, and he was persistent in continuing the search.

On that Saturday evening in the early summer of 2020, I received the results of dendrochronology—the science of using growth patterns in trees to date building framing—that had been performed on samples taken from two posts, a brace, and floor joists in the building. The Oxford Tree Ring Laboratory in Maryland provided conclusive dates for four samples, and three were intact enough to determine a felling season: the winter of 1759–1760 and the spring of 1760.

The Williamsburg Bray School began operating in the building on September 29, 1760.

Now we knew. We had found the oldest existing building in England's North American colonies dedicated to educating enslaved and free Black children. But really, when we saw the original frame of the building in 2020, we knew even then that we were dealing with something special.

This building, as it turned out, was very different from what we assumed it would be. A February 16, 1769, letter written by Robert Carter Nicholas, trustee for the Williamsburg Bray School, wrote that teacher Ann Wager "continued in it [the building], as long as it was tenantable." Interpreted as a condition issue, it fit an assumption that a structure used as a school for Black children would be old, in bad condition, and of little use for other purposes.

This structure was brand new when the school began operating in it. A modern style for the period, it featured plastered walls complete with trim, fireplaces in all rooms, and six dormers to light the upstairs. This was a structure of the type that the vast majority of middle-class Williamsburg residents lived in during the second half of the eighteenth century.

The building communicated clear and vital links between the documentary and physical evidence, revealing clues about a piece of the world seen daily by many—an environment in which the students were taught, and in which the teacher lived. This provided critical components in understanding this important part of history.

When we first saw the building in 2020, it was largely encased in twentieth-century additions. The building was likely saved in the 1920s so it could be used as a dormitory for Methodist women attending William & Mary. It was during this time that the first major additions to the structure occurred. The changes during this period resulted in the removal of the original 1760 plaster; removal of much of the trim, windows, and doors; and a complete change to the roof line. When such dramatic changes occur, information about what the original building looked like is usually lost. After sorting through the changes and evidence, what the

Colonial Williamsburg preservation team found was astounding.

Most of the changes occurred in the period just before or during the Great Depression—a time of thrift and recycling. The team found original elements of the 1760 school reused throughout the structure. Sorting through every splinter, the team found original sections of chair rail, base board, a door, two window sashes, shingles, plaster lath, and many other details thought lost.

These pieces told us about the details of the building, original molding profiles, paint colors, and construction techniques.

But they also represent people and their stories, which often do not survive in the written record. *Fingerprints in bricks left by those who produced them. A nail slid into a gap in the stair by an unknown carpenter to stop it from squeaking. The wear patterns left behind by those that used the building. The thousands of touches necessary to round the original squared edges of the stair newel post. The thousands of footsteps that wore the floorboards and stair treads that are still evident today.*

The building shifted quickly from one believed to have been heavily altered with its original detailing and stories lost, to a remarkably intact building that willingly told its story. It was sharing the story of everyone who had worked on and used the building during its lifetime.

That the building exists today is a matter of good construction and good luck. It was originally located away from the center of Williamsburg and sat just outside the twentieth-century restoration of the colonial capital. William & Mary found a variety of uses for it, including housing for professors, a dormitory, and finally the home of the university's ROTC program.

In February 2023, this building, where enslaved and free Black students were taught reading, sewing, and tenets of the Anglican church, was moved for the second time. Now located at the corner of Nassau and Francis streets, the preservation of this important part of history began. Four months later, we completed vital structural repairs and slowly and carefully lowered the building 11½ inches to its new foundation. This was a prelude to the restoration work that serves as a touchpoint for research, scholarship, and conversation about race, religion, and education in America.

The research and discoveries about this building inform its restoration. The house itself was generous in answering our questions, starting with the dendrochronology results and later as our team carefully stripped away and examined the layers that had been added over time. The Williamsburg Bray School building revealed its secrets in such detail that the stories just came pouring out. It is in these details that we ensure that truth is told as we reveal a part of history that was hidden in plain sight.

Matthew Webster is the executive director of the Grainger Department of Architectural Preservation and Research for The Colonial Williamsburg Foundation, where he oversees the preservation of more than 600 structures in the National Landmark Historic District, the 18,000-piece architectural fragment collection, architectural research, and historic interiors. A former director at historic sites in Charleston, South Carolina, and Fredericksburg, Virginia, he consults nationally and internationally on eighteenth-century architecture and sits on preservation boards in the United States and the Caribbean. Webster oversees the architectural investigations and restoration of the Williamsburg Bray School.

MECKLENBURG, *September* 3, 1774.

RUN away from the Subscriber, about two Months ago, a likely Mulatto Lad named ISAAC BEE, formerly the Property of the late President *Blair*, and is well known about *Williamsburg*, where I am informed he has been several Times seen since his Elopement. He is between eighteen and nineteen Years of Age, low of Stature, and thinks he has a Right to his Freedom, because his Father was a Freeman, and I suppose will endeavour to pass for one. He can read, but I do not know that he can write; however, he may easily get some One to forge a Pass for him. I cannot undertake to describe his Apparel, as he has a Variety, and it is probable he may have changed them. Whoever apprehends the said Slave and delivers him to me, or to Mrs. *Burwell*, in *Williamsburg*, shall have 40 s. All Masters of Vessels are forewarned from carrying him out of the Country.

LEWIS BURWELL.

One Scholar's Story: Isaac's Homecoming

By Antonio T. Bly

Blessed is he that readeth...
–Revelation 1:3

Isaac Bee had had enough. Sometime in July of 1774, the "eighteen or nineteen" year old, named for Abraham's second born, gathered the few things he believed he had owned and stole away. As he made the long trek home, from Mecklenburg County, Virginia, to Williamsburg, he pondered the consequences of his brazen actions.

Surely, he might have thought to himself, he would be beaten for running away. If not beaten, he imagined the agony of the hot iron. In his Virginia, pain had been a prerequisite, one codified as a matter of statute, for those persons of his status.

During his flight, he might have also even contemplated the burgeoning politics of the day in which white Virginians had begun imagining themselves as slaves of their king.

Of the many details that Lewis Burwell, a planter, a member of the House of Burgesses, and Isaac Bee's new master, would document in a bulletin that appeared in the *Virginia Gazette* for Bee's apprehension, the most striking had been his reference about the fugitive's education.

"He can read," the stunned grandee reported, "I do not know that he can write; however, he may easily get some One to forge a Pass for him."

Well before Bee had even been conceived, most enslaved African Americans were denied access to education. Learning, in the minds of most owners, threatened the institution of slavery. By providing the enslaved with the tools through which they could steal away, reading, spelling, and writing undercut the authority of their enslavers. Purportedly, it also made them unruly and saucy.

And yet, Isaac Bee learned.

Other documents, however, reveal the story behind the ambiguous nature of Burwell's observation. Before becoming the property of the Mecklenburg enslaver, Isaac was taught by his father, a free Black man named John Inscoe Bee, who had been schooled by a Quaker, Flemming Bates.

In keeping with the Apostle Timothy's injunction, to "give attendance to reading, to exhortation, to doctrine" until Christ returned, John's son was enrolled at age ten in the Williamsburg Bray School for Negro Children. There, he learned "the Apostle's Creed, the Lord's Prayer, and the Ten Commandments." He learned "the true Spelling of Words." He learned how to "read distinctly."

Under the instruction of Ann Wager, who was the school's mistress for fourteen years, Bee also likely learned how to write, perhaps using one of the slate pencils unearthed during initial archaeological study of the original Bray School site.

Each Sunday, before he completed his education, Isaac Bee and the other members of his class attended Bruton Parish church where they were included as members of the Anglican congregation.

Consequently, after four years, Isaac proved himself a studious pupil which might explain, at least in part, why his sisters, Clara and Johanna, had been enrolled in the school in 1769.

Besides Isaac's homecoming, this volume celebrates the history and the legacies of the Williamsburg Bray School. Between 1760 and 1774, upwards of 400, if not more considering the school's injunction that its scholars practice their lessons at home, enslaved and free African Americans learned to read, spell, and write.

In this collection of essays, written by historians, professors, students, and several members of the Descendant Community, the complex story of Black communities is revealed.

INTRODUCTION

Indeed, within the pages of this modest tome emerges a rich history of people, like Isaac Bee, his sisters Clara and Johanna, and many others, rising, thriving, persevering, helping one another—up from slavery to freedom.

Antonio T. Bly, PhD, is the Peter H. Shattuck Endowed Chair in Colonial American History at California State University, Sacramento.

Sir,

Wmsburg, Virginia Feb. 16. 1761.

I receiv'd some Time ago a Letter from Mr. Franklin, informing me that I had been nominated as one of the Mannagers of a School to be erected here, for the Education of Negroes in the Christian Faith, &c. — Mr. Dawson, Commissary and Minister of this Parish, received at the same Time your Letter, on the same Subject. We consulted together and agreed with Mrs. Anne Wager for the opening a School at Michaelmas last, which was accordingly done. — We judg'd that the Allowance of £20 Sterling was not sufficient, we gave the Mistress therefore the whole Sum as a Salary, and Mr. Dawson undertook to raise Ten Pounds Sterling by Subscription for the Payment of House Rent: But he dying soon after, nothing has been done to that Purpose, neither do I believe did he ever answer your Letter. — I should have done it sooner myself, but I could not, 'til lately, procure your Letter of his Executor.

As I did not approve of raising the additional Money, by a petty Subscription, I have not attempted it, but am myself liable for the present Year. — I judg'd it more to the Credit of

Legacies of the Williamsburg Bray School

By Maureen Elgersman Lee and Nicole Brown

Seven key archival documents of correspondence between the Associates of Dr. Bray and the trustees of the Williamsburg Bray School serve as the backbone of this book and sketch the founding, operation, and closing of the Bray School between 1760 and 1774. They include three teacher reports that collectively name the 86 known Bray School students, most enslaved and some free.

These documents also serve as the foundation for the essays that comprise each chapter and constitute the book's essence. Written by Descendant Community members—who trace ancestry to Bray School attendees or to the broader Williamsburg community of the time—William & Mary undergraduate students and faculty, Colonial Williamsburg Foundation professionals, and other institutional and community leaders, these original essays serve as sites for reflection and analysis on the past and present of Black history, education, and community in Williamsburg, Virginia. The essays are joined together by the themes of discovery and community, as interpreted by a dynamic group of contributors who come with their own experiences, perspectives, and relationships to the Williamsburg Bray School. We asked these contributors to partner with us, and in doing so they bravely laid bare their thoughts, opinions, and emotions.

As seen in the three student lists known to survive—for 1762, 1765, and 1769—tavern keepers, carpenters, doctors, merchants, wig makers, blacksmiths, and members of Virginia's elite were among the male and female enslavers who utilized the Williamsburg Bray School according to their consciences and purposes. This information begs the questions: What kinds of labor were the enslaved children of these men and women expected to perform after their time at the Bray School? How did the education at this school influenced the hidden craftsmanship of Black hands in eighteenth-century Virginia?

There may never be answers to these questions. However, exploring letters and student lists which appear in this book allows for deeper investigations into our shared past.

Lost to colonial historiography for two centuries and the object of twentieth-century modifications, the Williamsburg Bray School structure was rumored to still exist in the early twenty-first century. All speculation was finally put to rest when in 2020, at the height of a global pandemic, dendrochronology testing confirmed the identity of the building standing on the William & Mary campus.

Since that time, historians, descendants, students, faculty, and visitors have engaged with the rebuilding and reimagination of the Williamsburg Bray School structure as it was being transformed from an undergraduate dormitory into an interpreted eighteenth-century building with a permanent home within Colonial Williamsburg's Historic Area. Some questions have been definitively answered, but further exploration continues into the legacies of Virginia's first official school for African American children. Amidst all this activity, scholarship, and debate, one foundational idea reverberates: the role of place in harnessing the transformative power of storytelling.

Stepping through the front door of the Williamsburg school's first home, a humble 17′ x 33′ structure, visitors are captivated by historical imagination as much as construction. The Williamsburg Bray School enables people from all backgrounds to discover how Williamsburg's diverse eighteenth-century community navigated intersections of race, status, education, faith, and agency. The building bears witness to this fact through the conversations it has inspired locally, nationally, and internationally.

The Williamsburg Bray School was as an educational enterprise, a site of resistance and resilience, and a physical structure.

We hope that the work of this book will inspire you to make new discoveries of your own about the school, students, and community of eighteenth-century Williamsburg. The path by which people can learn and appreciate the incredible depth of this history is a shared effort that spans generations, demographics, disciplines, and expertise. In this way, our book is an extension of that history and an avenue for more deeply understanding the legacies of the Williamsburg Bray School.

Founders of the Williamsburg Bray School: The Associates of Dr. Bray

The legacy of Black education associated with the Williamsburg Bray School starts almost forty years prior to the institution's opening in colonial Virginia. The Bray School was funded primarily by the Associates of Dr. Bray, a Church of England charitable institution, and supplemented by the private funds of local and international trustees. The Associates of Dr. Bray, known informally as the Bray Associates, had a mission to provide Anglican religious instruction to children of African and Indigenous descent in North America.

The Associates were founded on January 15, 1724, by the Rev. Dr. Thomas Bray. Born in Marton, Shropshire, in the latter part of the seventeenth century, Thomas Bray eventually became a key influencer in how religious texts and ideas would be spread across the British Empire. After getting his initial degree at the University of Oxford in 1678, Bray moved to various parishes. Rising in the ministerial ranks, Thomas Bray's first catechetical lectures, *A Course of Lectures upon the Church Catechism*, were composed in 1696. Bray eventually passed away on February 15, 1730, after spending more than fifty years in religious public life.

Rev. Dr. Thomas Bray founded several Anglican charities prior to his establishment of the Associates of Dr. Bray. Bray founded the Society for the Propagation of the Gospel in Foreign Parts (SPG), meant to send Anglican missionaries across the empire, and the Society for the Promotion of Christian Knowledge (SPCK), whose primary focus was establishing charity schools in England and publishing books on the principles of Christian religion. Based on a variety of religious records, Bray's investment in the Church of England's expansion was apparent. His mission to augment Anglican religious education led to the formation of the Associates of Dr. Bray.

The Associates were founded in part through Bray's work, but also through his partnership with Abel Tassin, Sieur D'Allonne (also D'Allone). As secretary to Princess Mary of Orange—later Queen Mary—and to King William III, D'Allonne wielded power and influence. While not much is known about the relationship between D'Allonne and Bray, they had discussed collective hopes for the religious conversion and education of Black people in America, both enslaved and free, early in Bray's career. In 1717, D'Allonne decided to give Bray money for the purpose of furnishing a missionary to South Carolina to help convert Black people to the Church of England.

After his death in 1721, D'Allonne left one-tenth of his English estate to Bray for the purpose "of Erecting a School or Schools for the thorough Instructing in the Christian Religion the Young Children of Negro Slaves & such of their Parents as shew themselves inclinable & desirous to be so Instructed." Although the organization was not particularly active between 1724 and 1729, it regularly began meeting in the 1730s. Through religious instruction, the Bray Associates thought the education of free and enslaved Black children should "have a very good effect upon their [morals?] & make them faithful & honest in their Masters Service." The intent behind a Bray School education, according to the Associates' records, would be that the Black student should be seen but not heard; obedience and subjugation were key aims of instruction regardless of whether the child was held in bondage or not.

The Williamsburg Bray School, 1760–1774:
A Brief History

Despite its founders' prescriptive intent, the Williamsburg Bray School has a rich and varied history that highlights the often-fraught relationships between religion, race, slavery, and education in colonial Virginia. Operating between September 29, 1760, and August 20, 1774, the Williamsburg Bray School was one of five prominent Bray schools officially established in the colonial United States for Black students. The others operated in Philadelphia; New York City; Newport, Rhode Island; and Fredericksburg, Virginia. Other Bray schools were later established in Nova Scotia and the Caribbean.

A multitude of primary sources provides information about both how and why this institution was founded while simultaneously offering insight into the enslaved and free Black children who were instructed there. Most of what we know about the year-to-year operations of the Bray School comes from a vast, yet incomplete, collection of surviving documents: correspondence between local trustees in Williamsburg and Bray Associates' agents in London.

Based on these documents, we know that the girls and boys who attended the Bray School were approximately between three and ten years of age when they matriculated sometime over the school's fourteen years of operation. Some attended for a few years, others for a few months, and yet others, likely somewhere in between. In sum, upwards of 300 children likely passed through the doors of the school.

Through the school's only teacher, Ann Wager, the Williamsburg Bray School immersed children in the Anglican religion and provided basic instruction in reading, spelling, and etiquette for all students—and reserved additional instruction in sewing and knitting for girls.

The Williamsburg Bray School curriculum was rooted in a carefully curated collection of religious and practical texts endorsed and sometimes even authored by the Bray Associates themselves. The Bray Associates' ultimate ambition was to provide religious instruction to convert and assimilate students to Anglican Christian practice while still upholding the institution of slavery. However, subsequent records suggest that students used this education to expand their worlds in ways that directly contradicted the institution of slavery and its inherent attempt to dehumanize Black men, women, and children.

To understand the community of the Williamsburg Bray School, it is imperative to focus our attention on those who shaped and were shaped by the day-to-day operations of this institution. The 1762 school regulations and the various iterations of letters between Williamsburg and London consistently refer to the children as "scholars," a term which elevates the purported piety of the Bray Associates' mission. The title of scholar also seems to signify at least a moderate belief in the children's intellectual and performative capacities in a world where race-based theories of Black intellectual inferiority were rapidly gaining ground. However, the Bray Associates' need to see a spiritual return on their economic investment is also palpable across a larger body of letters. The term, scholar, signals that Bray School students were participants in the benefactor-beneficiary relationship inherent in the Bray Associates' model and part of a power relationship to which they did not consent. To honor the students and their descendants, and to reclaim the power of that title, contributing authors have continued the use of the term throughout this collection.

Most of the Bray School Scholars are not known to us by name. However, names of 86 individuals associated with the school have survived in the written record. They are:

John. Anne. William. Dick. Matt. Harry. London. Aggy. Shropshire. Young. Mary. Sally. Sukey. Aberdeen. Mary. Harry. George. Bristol. Aggy. Roger. Sam. Mary. Nancy. Judy. Ratchel.

Rippon. Jerry. Joseph. Dick. Jenny. Robert. Lucy. Elizabeth. Grace. George. Nanny. Locust. Mary Anne. Mary Jones. Elisha Jones. Sarah. Hannah. Sarah. John. Phoebe. Jane. John. Doll[y]. Elizabeth. Fanny. Isaac Bee. Catherine. Johanna Bee. Nancy. Clara Bee. Jack. Edmund. Johnny. Sal. Jack. Sally. Charlotte. Jenny. Jack. Dennis. Mourning. Joseph. Davy. Molly. Nancy. Davy. Phillis. Patt. Jack. James. Sal. Charles. Betty. Sylvia. Squire. Elizabeth. Harry Ashby. John Ashby. Mary Ashby. Adam. Fanny.

Born during the early eighteenth century, Ann Wager appears in various surviving colonial records, but her motivations for participating in the Bray School are not entirely clear. However, the Associates of Dr. Bray commended her "diligence and fidelity" in maintaining the school to their educational standards. Given this, it appears likely that in her classroom, Ann Wager was fully supportive of the pro-slavery motivations of the Associates of Dr. Bray.

The trustees of the Williamsburg Bray School also identified themselves as staunchly supportive of the colonialist and imperialist ideologies of the Bray Associates. Between 1760 and 1774, four trustees, with distinct tenures, managed and engaged with the Bray School. These men were Thomas Dawson (1760), William Hunter (1760–1761), William Yates (1761–1764), and Robert Carter Nicholas (1761–1774).

Rev. Thomas Dawson was rector of Bruton Parish, commissary (ecclesiastical administrator) to the Bishop of London, member of the Governor's Council, and president of William & Mary.

William Hunter published the *Virginia Gazette* and during his lifetime held a variety of notable positions: public printer to the Virginia colony, deputy postmaster general for the British North American colonies, and justice of the peace for York County.

Rev. William Yates succeeded Thomas Dawson as president of William & Mary, was a member of the Governor's Council, and served as rector of Bruton Parish.

Robert Carter Nicholas was a member of the House of Burgesses before being appointed treasurer for the Virginia colony in 1766, a position he held during his entire tenure as a Bray School trustee.

While all men had incredible power and reach, Robert Carter Nicholas was the longest-serving trustee; through his letters we know most about the operation of the Williamsburg Bray School.

In London, Rev. John Waring was the primary correspondent to Williamsburg Bray School trustees. Waring served as the Bray Associates' secretary between 1754 and 1779, corresponding with dozens of different individuals across a global network of Bray schools and libraries. Waring is a key figure in the collection and dissemination of information associated with Black education in the British Atlantic. While he is not particularly well known by the public or scholars today, it is impossible to ignore the role he played in the documents connected to the Williamsburg Bray School.

Records associated with the previously mentioned individuals make it apparent that education writ large was a controversial topic in the eighteenth-century Atlantic World. Before its first student had even crossed the school's threshold in September 1760, the Williamsburg Bray School ignited debate about the value and intention of Black education. Communal and individual reactions to this school continued to surprise, confound, and frustrate those working with the Bray School across its fourteen-year duration. With the school's 1774 closing due to the death of Ann Wager, the rise of tensions within the British Empire, and perhaps diminished practical returns on educational investment for enslavers, formal Anglo-Christian education for Black Virginians slowed via official means. Regardless, the impact of this school on Williamsburg and its diverse community continued to be felt. The hundreds of students educated at the school would study, seek agency, and find meaning through education long after the school closed its doors.

Williamsburg Bray School Chronology

February 1760 The Associates of the Late Dr. Bray, also known as the Bray Associates, in London, express their intensions to establish a school "for the Instruction of Negro Children in the Principles of the Christian Religion" in Williamsburg based on the recommendation of Benjamin Franklin.

September 1760 The Williamsburg Bray School opens. With Ann Wager as its teacher, the school enrolls twenty-four students, both girls and boys. The students receive religious instruction and are taught reading, spelling, and comportment. Girls are also taught to sew and knit. Research increasingly suggests that writing was also taught.

September 1762 Ann Wager's first known report of children at the Williamsburg Bray School names thirty students, ages three to ten. Twenty-seven children are enslaved; three are free.

December 1765 The second known report of children at school records the names of thirty-four students. Thirty-two children are enslaved; two are free. No ages are recorded. That same month, the Williamsburg Bray School moves to a larger building owned by John Blair Sr., president of the Governor's Council and member of the Board of Visitors for William & Mary.

INTRODUCTION

April 1768   The Bray Associates request more information on the progress of the Williamsburg Bray School as tensions arise around the school's budget.

February 1769   The third known report of students at school names thirty children. Twenty-eight children are enslaved; two are free. No ages are recorded.

December 1772   No school report is available, due to the teacher's "Indisposition" and the trustee's engagement in a "variety of public Business."

August 1774   Ann Wager dies. The Williamsburg Bray School closes, pending further direction from the Bray Associates.

April 1777   The American Revolution causes the Bray Associates to cease all support of Bray schools in the American colonies—including Williamsburg.

June 2020   Dendrochronology testing confirms that the original Bray School building is located at 524 Prince George Street on the campus of William & Mary.

February 2021   The discovery of the Williamsburg Bray School and the launch of the Williamsburg Bray School Initiative, a partnership between William & Mary and the Colonial Williamsburg Foundation, are announced.

October 2021   The William & Mary Bray School Lab is officially launched.

February 2023   The Colonial Williamsburg Foundation relocates the Williamsburg Bray School building from the William & Mary campus to its permanent home on the corner of Nassau and Francis streets, in Colonial Williamsburg's Historic Area.

November 2024   The Colonial Williamsburg Foundation opens the restored Williamsburg Bray School building to the public with new interpretation and programming.

Bray School Student Residences

1. Adam (1769), Fanny (1769)
2. Charlotte (1769)
3. Mourning (1769)
4. Jane (1762), John (1762), Dolly (1762), Doll, (1765), Elizabeth (1765), Fanny (1765), Isaac Bee (1765), Catherine (1765), Johanna Bee (1765, 1769), Nancy (1769), Clara Bee (1769)
5. Jenny (1769), Jack (1769)
6. Dennis (1769)
7. Mary (1762), Harry (1762)
8. Hannah (1762, 1765), Sarah (1769)
9. Robert (1762), Lucy (1762)
10. Mary (1762), Nancy (1769), Judy (1769), Ratchel (1769)
11. John (1762), Patt (1765), Jack (1765), James (1765), Sal (1765)
12. Aggy (1762), Roger (1762, 1765), Sam (1765, 1769)
13. Rippon (1762), Jenny (1765)
14. Sylvia (1765)
15. London (1762), Aggy (1762), Shropshire (1762), Young (1765), Mary (1765, 1769), Sally (1769), Sukey (1769)

16. Molly (1765)
17. George (1762), Bristol (1762)
18. George (1762), Nanny (1765)
19. Nancy (1765), Davy (1765)
20. Phoebe (1762), Jerry (1769), Joseph (1769), Dick (1769)
21. Aberdeen (1762)
22. Edmund (1765), Johnny (1765), Jack (1769)
23. Phillis (1765)
24. Sally (1769)
25. Squire (1765)
26. Sal (1765), Jack (1769)

Bray School Locations

A. Williamsburg Bray School (1760-1765)
B. Possible location of second Williamsburg Bray School (1766-1774)

To learn more information and to see a detailed map visit: colonialwilliamsburg.org/bray

Records and Reflections

The essays that follow explore a variety of perspectives on the establishment of an 18th-century school for Black children in Virginia, and its meaning for the students and the community—then and now. Some essays are products of years of research and writing on the Williamsburg Bray School; others represent more recent opportunities to reflect on the school and its historical context. All reflect on the enduring legacies of what became known as the Williamsburg Bray School.

As we considered the components to include in this book, it was the absences that stood out. The voices of the Associates of Dr. Bray and the school's administrators are present in the seven letters that trace the arc of the Williamsburg Bray School's evolution. But the voices of the students are silent. For this reason, it was important to include the voices of the community—in particular, the descendants of the Williamsburg Bray School Scholars. The contributors' words, reflections, opinions, and questions are their own. They were neither influenced by nor do they necessarily reflect the opinions of the editors or the institutions they represent. While no one can replace the voices lost to history, the diverse group of essayists in this section call on us to remember these students, to identify them, and to continue searching for their truth, and that is our charge.

London Feb: 29: 1760

Rev.d Sir

   I am desired by a Society who call themselves The Associates of the Late D.r Bray (the Objects of whose Attention are the Conversion of the Negroes in the British Plantations, founding Parochial Libraries & other good purposes) to acquaint You that lately agreed to open a School at Williamsburg in Virginia for the Instruction of Negro Children in the Principles of the Christian Religion. They earnestly request that You M.r Hunter, Postmaster & the Minister of the Parish will be so kind as to assist them in the Prosecution of this pious Undertaking, & that You will with all convenient Speed open a School for this purpose: & as 'tis probable that Some of Each Sex may be sent for Instruction, The Associates are therefore of opinion that a Mistress will be preferable to a Master as She may teach the Girls to Sew knit &c. as well as all to Say their Catechism. They think 30 Children or thereabouts will sufficiently employ one person, & therefore would at present confine their School to about that Number. I need not inform You that it is their Desire the Expence may be as small as the Nature of the Design & proper Incouragement of it will admit. I hope 15 £ or 16£ a Year may suffice, but desire You will not exceed 20£ Sterling. They are unwilling to suppose that any persons in Your Province will disapprove of this pious Undertaking, but hope that all Objections will be silenced by the School's being put under the Care & Patronage of such

ONE

Establishing the Williamsburg Bray School, 1760–1761

*Rev. John Waring to Rev. Thomas Dawson,
February 29, 1760*

*William Hunter to Bray Associates,
February 16, 1761*

As secretary of the Associates of Dr. Bray, English minister John Waring was on a mission to establish schools in colonial America that would provide a religious education for enslaved and free Black children. On February 29, 1760, Rev. Waring wrote to Rev. Thomas Dawson, William & Mary's president and rector of Bruton Parish Church, to tell him of plans to establish such a school in Williamsburg. Dawson wielded significant power and influence and was considered essential to securing a Bray school in Virginia's colonial capital. It was Waring's responsibility to initiate and maintain correspondence between the Bray Associates in London and prospective and established Bray School trustees in the British colonies.

Waring shared the rationale behind establishing a Bray school in Williamsburg, highlighted tentative aspects of the curriculum, and listed the contents of a box to be delivered that contained no less than 235 books intended for classroom study at the still-to-be established school. This methodology was a signature of the Bray Associates' operations, and proved successful in affecting the establishment of a school in Williamsburg and other American cities.

Dating through dendrochronology shows that while Waring was reaching out to Williamsburg's colonial elite to put the Associates' plans into action, trees used to build the tenement building that would house the Williamsburg Bray School were being felled, cut, and readied to take their place in history.

Waring's letter is one of two important pieces of correspondence about the school's beginning. The second letter, dated February 16, 1761, was written by William Hunter. In addition to his role as the Virginia colony's official printer, Hunter was also one of two deputy postmaster generals for British North America. The other was Benjamin Franklin, who, as a member of the Associates of Dr. Bray, had suggested Williamsburg as a potential location for a school. In his letter to the Associates, Hunter conveyed two important developments of late 1760: the September opening of the Williamsburg Bray School and the November death of Thomas Dawson, who, along with Hunter, had played an essential role in launching the school and hiring its teacher, Ann Wager. Hunter explained that before Dawson passed away, he had helped lay the groundwork for the first official school for Black students in Williamsburg. These letters are two of the most critical surviving pieces of correspondence that help document the early history of the Williamsburg Bray School. Tragically, neither Dawson nor Hunter lived beyond 1761, but they did accept the Bray Associates' charge to establish the Bray School by serving as its first trustees.

The essays that follow reflect upon two seminal documents that signal the Williamsburg Bray School's beginnings.

Letter Transcript
Rev. John Waring to Rev. Thomas Dawson

London Feb: 29. 1760

Rev^d. Sir

I am desired by a Society who call themselves The Associates of the Late D^r. Bray (the Objects of whose Attention are the Conversion of the Negroes in the British plantations, founding Parochial Libraries & other good Purposes) to acquaint You that they lately agreed to open a School at Williamsburg in Virginia for the Instruction of Negro Children in the Principles of the Christian Religion. They earnestly request that You M^r. Hunter, Postmaster & the Minister of the Parish will be so kind as to assist them in the Prosecution of this pious Undertaking, that you will with all convenient speed open a School for this purpose: & As 'tis probable that some of each Sex may be sent for Instruction, The Associates are therefore of opinion that a Mistress will be preferable to a Master as she may teach the Girls to Sew knit & as well as <u>all</u> to ˄read & Say their Catechism. They think 30 Children or thereabout will sufficiently employ one person & therefore wou'd at present confine their School to about that number. I need not inform You that it is their Desire, the Expence may be as small as the nature of the Design & proper Encouragement of it will admit. Hope 15£ or 16£ a year may suffice, but desire you will not exceed 20£ Sterling. They are unwilling to suppose that any persons in your Province will disapprove of this pious Undertaking, but hope that all Objections will be Silenced by the School & being put under the Care &

Patronage of Such persons & that all prejudices against instructing the Negroes will gradualy die away, as 'tis hoped the good Effects of this School will every day become more & more apparent.

The Associates presuming on Your Kind Assistance have Sent a Box of Books for the use of the School, besides which there is a Folio Volume, a present from the Associates to Your College Library. There are likewise 5 Copies of M^r. Bacons sermons on this subject which may be useful to lend to Such Masters who do not seem Sufficiently apprized how much it is their Duty to take Care that their slaves especially those born in their house be instructed in the principles of Christianity.

I am directed to request the favour of a Letter from You as soon as the School is opened, & that You will from time to time send us an account of the State of the School, the number of each Sex admitted, the Progress they make in their Reading & Catechism &c.

About a year & Quarter ago a School was opened at Philadelphia for 30 black Children on the Associates Account; which met with a very Favourable Reception. The Desire of the Masters to have their black Children instructed. The Progress the Children have made & their decent behaviour give great Satisfaction: That School is under the Care & Inspection of the Rev^d. M^r. Sturgeon: who requires the Mistress to attend the Children to Church on Wed^s. & Frid & after divine service he charitably catechises & instructs them.

M^r. Franklin of Philadelphia One of the Associates & at present in London intends to write to M^r. Hunter on this subject, which He probably will receive about the time this comes to your hands Be pleased to draw on me for the salary half yearly or Quarterly as is most convenient: & Acquaint me from time to time What supply of Books may be wanting for the use of the Children. Be pleased to direct to me at M^r. Birds Bookseller at the Angel & Bible in Ave Mary Lane near S^t. Paul's London: That God may bless & prosper Your Endeavours to the advancement of his own Glory is the hearty Prayer of.

Rev^d. Sir
Your most obedient
humble Servt.
J^n. War[ing]

Books in the Box

50 Childs first Book

40 English Instructor

25 Catechism broke &c

10 Easy method of instructing Youth

3 Indian instructed

2 Preliminary Essays

5 Bacons 4 Sermons

5 Bacons 2 Sermons to Negroes

10 Christians Guide

3 Church Catechism with text of Scrip.

} The Box was intrusted to M^r. Franklin's who (I believe) consign'd it to M^r. Hunter.

12 friendly Admonitions

70 Sermons before Trustees & Associates

Letter Transcript
William Hunter to Bray Associates

W^{ms}burg, Virginia Feb. 16. 1761.

Sir.

I received some Time ago a Letter from M^r. Franklin, informing me that I had been nominated as one of the Mannagers of a School to be erected here, for the Education of Negroes in the Christian Faith, &c. —M^r. Dawson, Commissary and Minister of this Parish, receiv'd at the same Time your Letter, on the same Subject. We consulted together and agreed with M^{rs}. [Ann] Wager for the opening a School at Michaelmas last; which was accordingly done. —We judg'd that the Allowance of £20 Sterling was not Sufficient, we gave the Mistress therefore the whole Sum as a Salary, and M^r. Dawson undertook to raise Ten Pounds Sterling by Subscription for the Payment of House Rent: But he dying soon after, nothing has been done to that Purpose, neither do I believe did he ever answer your Letter. —I should have done it sooner myself, but I could not, 'til lately, procure your Letter of his Executor.

As I did not approve of raising the additional Money, by a petty Subscription, I have not attempted it, but am myself liable for the present Year. —I judg'd it more to the Credit of the Associates to pay the whole Expence necessary, than to be aided by a trifling Contribution. —I would therefore recommend it to them to increase the Allowance to £30 Sterling, if they would maintain the School in any tolerable Credit. —And this I think is as little as it can be done for.

I have the Pleasure of informing the associates that their Design has been generally well receiv'd.

The School ~~has~~ was opened with 24 Scholars, (as many I think as one Woman can well manage) Their Progress and Improvement in So Short a Time, has greatly exceeded my Expectation, and I have Reason to hope that the good Intentions of the Associates will be fully answer'd, by the Care and good Conduct of the Mistress. —

At present I stand Single in this Undertaking but M^r. Yates being last Week elected Minister of the Parish in the Room of M^r. Dawson, I shall communicate to him your Letter, and doubt not his Concurrence. — As it was the Intention of the Associates to nominate three Trustees, not knowing that M^r. Dawson was Minister of the Parish, I would recommend a Letter to be written to Robt. Carter Nicholas Esqr. to whom I have never mention'd it, imagining that a Letter from the Associates would best secure his Compliance.

The Mistress was paid one Quarter's Salary at Christmas, for which I have given M^r. Tarpley an Order on you, but may probably for the future draw but once a Year, to prevent the Trouble of small Bills.

Be pleas'd to assure the Associates of my hearty Endeavours to further their good Designs, by making this Establishment, at present in its Infancy, as generally beneficial as possible.

I am, respectfully, Sir,

Your very h^{ble} Servt.
W^m. Hunter

M^r. John Waring
at M^r. Bird's, Bookseller at the Angel & Bible of
   Ave Mary Lane London

Preparing to Open the Bray School on September 29, 1760

An essay by Julie Richter

In a letter written on February 29, 1760, Rev. John Waring of the Bray Associates directed Rev. Thomas Dawson and William Hunter to open a school for the religious education of Black children in Williamsburg. The Associates, as Waring wrote, believed "30 Children or thereabout will sufficiently employ one person," and this person should be a woman who could teach girls to sew and knit in addition to instructing all her scholars in Christianity. Waring wanted Dawson and Hunter to undertake this work "with all convenient speed" and advised that they should not spend more than £20 per year on this endeavor.

After requesting to be informed when the school opened, Waring did not comment on either the building or the children in the rest of his letter. He did not elaborate on the physical structure, an indication that the Bray Associates saw the school as an institution, not as a space in which girls and boys would gather for lessons from Ann Wager. Waring showed little interest in the children beyond the approximate number of boys and girls who would attend and a hope that they would make good progress in their lessons; these children were a group who, once they received instruction in Christianity, would know their proper place in Virginia's social hierarchy. In contrast, both the building that would house the school's operations and the children who would be the first scholars were of concern to Dawson and Hunter. Centering this structure and the scholars in the story of opening the

Williamsburg Bray School provides a window into the beginning of what the Bray Associates described as "a pious undertaking."

It is likely that Dawson and Hunter decided to begin their work by finding a building to rent for the school. During the 1750s, Williamsburg experienced a building boom that saw tradesmen construct new structures and remodel existing homes, taverns, and public buildings. The population also increased as prominent Virginians decided to move to the capital city. Hunter and Dawson knew rents were higher than Waring hoped they would spend, and they would not have looked for a building on Duke of Gloucester Street or Palace Green. A recently built structure on Prince George Street likely caught their attention because its location away from the city's main streets and vistas meant that the rent was lower than in other areas in Williamsburg. It is also possible that Dawson and Hunter rented this building because it was less visible to people who felt uneasy about the prospect of enslaved and free Black children becoming Christians and learning to read English.

In 2024, we do not know the names of the first children who attended the Williamsburg Bray School when it opened on September 29, 1760. On that morning, a group of twenty-four boys and girls, likely between three and ten years old, walked from their homes and entered the school building on Prince George Street. What was it like for these children to walk into the school? On that morning, when they crossed the threshold, they entered a center passage that measured seven feet by seventeen feet; the room to their left was some eleven feet by seventeen feet and the room to their right was a bit larger, measuring thirteen feet by seventeen feet. The recently completed structure likely smelled like a new building; the scholars would have noticed the smell of wood used to construct the framing and to cover the exterior. They might have felt crowded in the two main spaces Ann Wager used for instruction. If the first day of school was clear, sunlight would have streamed through the windows' glass panes and made it easier for children to see numbers and letters on the pages of the books as they began their lessons.

The act of entering this school building brought children from different households throughout the city into a single building. If they were strangers on that first morning, this quickly changed. Education was a communal experience for these girls and boys; they spent long hours with each other, seven days a week, at school and at church. Reading, often thought of as a solitary endeavor, was collaborative for these scholars as they learned their letters. They also shared the noises in the school—from the sounds of other children turning the pages in the books sent by the Bray Associates and reciting lessons to pins landing on the floor, thread being pulled through fabric, and slate pencils presumably scratching on the surface of slates. The scholars took information with them when they left the school building at the end of the day, extending the communal nature of learning to family and friends. Through the actions of the first twenty-four scholars, the Williamsburg Bray School extended throughout the city's enslaved and free Black population.

Julie Richter, PhD, is the director of the National Institute of American History & Democracy (NIAHD) at William & Mary and a member of the Harrison Ruffin Tyler Department of History. Richter teaches various classes, including Public History; Gender, Race, and Power; Seventeenth- and Eighteenth-Century Virginia; and Early America, and served as an Office of Strategic Cultural Partnerships Faculty Fellow.

Tensions in Expanding the Reach of Education: Reflections on the Past and Present

An essay by Jason A. Chen

I first started writing this reflection in April of 2023. Two months prior, on February 10, 2023, the Bray-Digges House, which originally housed the Williamsburg Bray School, was moved to a new site in Colonial Williamsburg's Historic Area. Moving this building and preparing it for the public to see will allow a larger audience to hear the stories of the Bray School and its students. I am also writing in June of 2023 when news headlines are flooded with reports about book and curriculum bans, where officials in some localities have removed books that deal with race and racism, or districts have banned the teaching of courses such as AP African American History. These efforts are happening all over the country, including in Virginia.

These two contexts inform my reflection on the Williamsburg Bray School because they reinforce the notion that education is *powerful*. On the one hand, William & Mary and The Colonial Williamsburg Foundation are working to center voices that have long been pushed to the margins. The students at the Williamsburg Bray School did not have the positionality to be the primary architects of their educational stories. Instead, those who created, funded, and managed the school could determine the narrative and continue to have a significant ability to do so through surviving documents. Education is *powerful*, but only if we broaden the participation of those who tell the stories. In this case, it is by centering the narratives of the Bray School Descendant Community.

This is the lens through which I view the February 29, 1760, letter from Rev. Waring to Rev. Dawson and the February 16, 1761, letter from William Hunter to the Bray Associates. In his 1760 letter, Rev. Waring acknowledged that the objectives of the Associates of the Late Dr. Bray were for "the conversion of the [N]egroes in the British plantations" as evidenced by the establishment of Bray schools, including one in Williamsburg. Confirming this purpose, the 1761 letter showed William Hunter also acknowledged that a school is "to be erected here, for the Education of Negroes in the Christian Faith." *Education is powerful.*

For the Bray Associates, they viewed education as a pathway toward salvation. But the Bray Associates were not naïve. They knew that educating Black children, the vast majority of whom were enslaved by wealthy white landowners, professionals, and colonial administrators, could face resistance. As Rev. Waring noted, he and the Bray Associates hoped that "all Objections will be silenced by the School" and "all prejudices against instructing the Negroes will [gradually] die away."

A year later, William Hunter, the official printer to the Virginia colony, in his 1761 letter to the Bray Associates indicated that, "[the Bray Associates'] Design has been generally well received" and "[the 24 Scholars'] Progress and Improvement in so short a Time, has greatly exceeded my Expectation." Given that the school continued for another thirteen years after the letter was written, one can only surmise that the instruction of enslaved and free Black children was sufficiently accepted by people who had the power to continue or discontinue it.

We also see the Bray Associates trying to broaden access to education within a society that included dissenting voices. Granted, they were still using scripture to instruct Black children about their inferior status and social station relative to white people. The fact that Black boys and girls were being formally educated while many white children were not, was remarkable.

There lies in Rev. Waring's 1760 letter the acknowledgment of significant resistance to the education of Black children, especially from wealthy white enslavers. As is the case with many parents and lawmakers wanting to constrain access to books and curriculum dealing with controversial topics including race and racism, most wealthy white enslavers in colonial Virginia also wanted to restrict education for fear of its power to potentially disrupt a social order that benefited some and disadvantaged others. As I reflect on this letter from Rev. Waring vis-à-vis the push and pull of today's debate over who gets access to what type of education, I am reminded of just how important it is to *engage* in our nation's processes, and that broadening the participation of a diverse electorate will lead to a stronger and more accountable democracy.

Jason A. Chen is a professor of educational psychology at the William & Mary School of Education who has also served as an Office of Strategic Cultural Partnerships Faculty Fellow. With a PhD in Educational Studies from Emory University and a post-doctoral research fellowship from Harvard University, he questions the variety of ways that emerging technologies can be used as tools for motivation, engagement, and learning.

Colonialism & Education:
Comparing the Brafferton Indian School and the Williamsburg Bray School

An essay by Fallon Burner

Would you be surprised to learn that there were crossovers and connections between the delivery of African American and Indigenous education in eighteenth-century Williamsburg? I was.

The letters of February 1760 and 1761, between the Bray Associates in London and local Bray School trustees in Williamsburg, highlight some similarities and differences between the Bray School, for Black girls and boys, and William & Mary's Brafferton School, for Indigenous boys, as it pertains to purpose, funding, and power.

Prior to having its own building beginning in 1723, the Brafferton Indian School was known as the "Boyle School" or simply the "Indian School," and operated primarily out of William & Mary's now iconic Wren Building as well as in the city of Williamsburg. Overall, dozens of boys of various ages are said to have been enrolled in this school between 1702 and 1778. Brafferton students came from Native Nations all over the Eastern Woodlands—a cultural and ecological zone covering roughly the eastern third of the United States today that stretches from the Arctic Circle to Florida and from the Mississippi River to the Atlantic Ocean. These students were likely the sons of chiefs or other diplomats and dignitaries. They were taught to read and write English and were exposed to the Anglican faith. Authorities at the Brafferton School knew that they were accountable to their Indigenous alliances both locally and on the frontier for their treatment of those nations' sons.

This was not the case for the Bray School, where enslaved parents had no political power and free Black parents did not fare much better. The February 1760 letter showed concern that the slaveholding community might oppose the idea of a school for Black children, but demonstrated optimism that it would work out. The Brafferton Indian School had the blessing of the Crown, and its place within a network of sophisticated alliances keeping Virginia safe ensured that the opinion of Williamsburg's residents about the Brafferton warranted comparatively less of their concern.

One of the Society for the Propagation of the Gospel in Foreign Parts' (SPG) biggest projects in the eighteenth century was the Brafferton Indian School. At least one scholar has posited that the Brafferton Indian School and the Williamsburg Bray School had a mutual funding source in the estate of Robert Boyle, the SPG's first president. The SPG had a hand in funding many "Indian" educational endeavors in the British colonies.

Both African and Native societies were viewed as "heathen" by the British population and government, mostly because they were not presumed Christian. Another word that the British often used to describe both peoples was "uncivilized," and this word, while still giving a nod to religion, had stronger tones of judgment for simply living in ways that seemed outside of the white, British cultural norm. While the British enslaved members of both populations, Indigenous enslavement in Virginia generally ended around the mid-eighteenth century, as the practice of Black enslavement was increasing exponentially and the British importation of Africans to the Americas was reaching its apex.

At both the Brafferton and the Bray School, students were taught by a single instructor. However, while the Brafferton schoolmaster was always male, the Bray Associates specifically requested a schoolmistress since sewing and knitting were to be taught in addition to the broader curriculum of reading and religious study for both girls and boys. The Bray School's teacher, Ann Wager, was an accomplished teacher-tutor, known locally, and seemingly well respected. We know that the Brafferton boys received the same education as any son of the wealthy elite who attended William & Mary, even if they were taught and housed separately.

The February 16, 1761, letter from William Hunter to the Bray Associates raised the issue of funding to pay and house Wager amid the high Williamsburg rents. The Bray Associates indicated that extra funds were to come out of the pockets of Williamsburg's citizens. That was not happening with the Indian School. Throughout the school's existence, clothing, school supplies, and even medical care were provided for its students. The British wanted to entice their communities to integrate more into British society. In its final era and in the transition from administration by the Crown to administration by the Virginia colony, Colonel and then Governor Patrick Henry authorized expenses for Wyandot citizen Henry Bawbee to wear fashionable—and, by some accounts, ostentatious—attire. While the British had not wanted to antagonize their Indigenous allies, Virginia's patriot government was actively wooing Indigenous allies to its side in the Revolution. While Wager was asking for money, the Indigenous students were well provided for.

Overall, the one unifying perspective of white British society was that Indigenous and Black communities needed to be enlightened by the "Gospel of Christ" as delivered by the Anglican Church. So, when one sees the Williamsburg Bray School, one also sees the Brafferton Indian School. (And vice versa.) In this way, the Brafferton Indian School and the Williamsburg Bray School were products of English colonial politics and religious philanthropy.

Fallon Burner is Indigenous Historian and Program Design Manager at The Colonial Williamsburg Foundation. A graduate of the University of California, Berkeley and the University of Saskatchewan's History programs, Burner's previous work on language revitalization and revival within the Wendat and Wyandot(te) nations has won multiple awards. As a native of Yorktown, Virginia, Burner is grateful to the Virginia tribes for their caretaking of these lands since time immemorial.

Revisiting the Williamsburg Bray School after Fifty Years

An essay by John C. Van Horne

I first encountered the Bray Associates fifty years ago, when I was a graduate student at the University of Virginia searching for a dissertation topic that had not yet been thoroughly explored. William W. Abbot, former William & Mary professor and editor of the *William & Mary Quarterly*, was my advisor. Several articles about the Associates of Dr. Bray and their work in the American colonies had appeared in the previous decades by such scholars as Carter G. Woodson, Edgar Legare Pennington, Richard I. Shelling, and Mary A. Stephenson, but the Associates' archive in London had not yet been edited and made accessible. I, therefore, undertook to edit and publish all the Associates' correspondence with their American representatives from the early 1730s until 1777, when their activities in the colonies ceased during the American Revolution. More recently I have, with Grant Stanton, documented the history of the school in Philadelphia—the only one to reopen following the Revolution—from 1758 until its closure in 1845.

Reading once again after a long hiatus, these two letters—to the Reverend Thomas Dawson and from William Hunter—documenting the beginnings of the Williamsburg Bray School proved to be quite enlightening. It was Benjamin Franklin, a member and soon-to-be chairman of the Associates, who in January 1760 recommended the men in Williamsburg, New York City, and Newport, Rhode Island, he thought most appropriate to superintend the proposed schools and most likely to accept the charge. I had never thought to question Franklin's recommendations, which in all cases were of Anglican ministers and prominent laymen. But his Williamsburg recommendations raise questions.

Dawson's plate was quite full, as he was not only rector of Bruton Parish Church, but also president of William & Mary, commissary of the Bishop of London, and a member of the Governor's Council. Perhaps unbeknownst to Franklin, Dawson was also embroiled in various controversies and around this time admitted to habitual drunkenness; he was dead by November 1760 at age 45. Yet as Dawson was the senior Anglican cleric in Williamsburg, Franklin could hardly have passed him over. William Hunter was well known to Franklin; they were fellow printers and deputy postmasters general for the American colonies, and they had traveled the country together on post office business in the mid-1750s. But Franklin knew that Hunter had been seriously ill and had sought treatment in England, from which he had just returned to Virginia in July 1759; he was dead two years later, still in his thirties.

Yet Franklin had it right. Both men did accept the charge, and within months they had hired Ann Wager as the school mistress. They opened the school successfully, with Hunter even bearing some of the initial expenses personally.

Waring's letter to Dawson is highly prescriptive. It specifies such details as the preferability of a mistress over a master, the ideal number of students (thirty), the curriculum (teaching "the Girls to Sew knit &c. as well as *all* to read & Say their Catechism"), and the approved annual expense (£20). In fact, these provisions hew closely to the suggestions Franklin made in a letter to Waring of February 17, 1758. Waring also spent a paragraph describing the Philadelphia school, which had been open for fifteen months at the time he wrote. Waring cited the "Favourable Reception" it met with, the "Desire of the Masters to have their black Children instructed," and the "Progress the Children have made." Waring (and Franklin) clearly believed that the same template would work equally well in both a metropolis in the North with many free Black children and a much smaller town in the South with a mostly enslaved Black population whose enslavers might well view the enterprise differently. Experience did not entirely bear this assumption out.

The list of books the Associates sent "for the Use of the School" includes titles appropriate for young pupils just embarking on an education and others that are clearly aimed at "Masters who do not seem Sufficiently apprized how much it is their Duty to take Care that their Slaves... be instructed in the principles of Christianity," such as the sermons of the Reverend Thomas Bacon. Those sermons to white enslavers, which the Associates also sent, complemented the ones Bacon delivered to the enslaved, admonishing them to obey their masters and mistresses in all things. That pair of sermons, by a native Briton transplanted to Maryland, in a way neatly encapsulates the ethos of the Church of England in the eighteenth century and therefore the Associates' operating assumptions about the conversion and education of Black children in America: a laudable mission that should be supported by white enslavers while never threatening to alter the temporal condition of the enslaved.

John C. Van Horne is director emeritus of the Library Company of Philadelphia, which he served for thirty years. He was educated at Princeton University and holds a PhD from the University of Virginia. He has published more than a dozen articles and has edited or co-edited numerous books, including Religious Philanthropy and Colonial Slavery: The American Correspondence of the Associates of Dr. Bray, 1717–1777 *and many volumes of* The Papers of Benjamin Henry Latrobe.

The Tentacles of the Williamsburg Bray School

An essay by Robert "Bobby" A. Braxton

Because I have the background of an engineer, I generally like to have my hands on things and feel like I have a good grasp of them. So, the first thing I wanted to do in reading the Williamsburg Bray School letters from February 29, 1760, and February 16, 1761, was to define who the people were and what their relationships were to each other. I have been reading the 1760 and 1761 letters back and forth, and up and down. And what did I think of the letters? There are some interesting players here, including Benjamin Franklin, John Waring, Thomas Dawson, and William Hunter.

The first letter seems to tell us that Benjamin Franklin had a lot of pull. I wonder what would have happened with the Williamsburg Bray School if he had not been involved. I do not think that the school would have been as prominent or would have enrolled as many students as it did. So, to me, Franklin was a major player, even though there are just a few words about him in these documents. I also wonder what the Bray Associates really had in mind for the students that they were attempting to educate. What were they really trying to do?

I often wonder about interviewing a few students, both male and female; I wish I could ask them so many questions. How did the children sound? How did they speak? How did they act? Did the children like the Bray School? Did they have anything they could truly call their own? Did they have a chance to play? I wonder what the children would say. School is a culture—no matter how good, bad, or indifferent. But we do not have the answers to these questions, or others, because it appears that no one asked the children how they felt or what they wanted.

The second letter, written a year after the first, talked about money. Money was very important in establishing and continuing the operation of the Bray School. In fact, money and finances represent a theme that runs throughout the school's history. You had Benjamin Franklin, so, therefore, you had money. Another thing to notice is that Rev. Waring, in London, was communicating with the trustees in Williamsburg quite a bit. They were getting down into the financial minutia, so to speak, to make sure that the Bray School moved forward. This required local trustees to take more of the money budgeted for the school and reserve it for the teacher, Ann Wager. In other words, they were playing musical money. Things have not changed too much. The 1700s are pretty much like the 2000s when it comes to following the money.

But suppose that the Williamsburg Bray School was never there. What would have happened to the enslaved and free children? There would have been a segment of the Black population who would have been uneducated—at least formally. Let us consider the math. Let us just say those first twenty-four children who attended the Williamsburg Bray School when it opened in 1760 grew up and established relationships. Then there were forty-eight people who more than likely could read and write. OK. So, you had those forty-eight people—and so on and so on. I mean, those original twenty-four students impacted by the Bray School must number at least 500 people today. But what would have happened if the Bray School had not come into being? You would have to erase a lot of that formal or informal education.

So, these are what I would call the tentacles of the Williamsburg Bray School.

Now, think about the Bray School Descendant Community more broadly and think about First Baptist Church. Do you know why everybody left Bruton Parish? Black people wanted their own place for singing their own songs and doing their own thing. How many of those people came through the Bray School? How many of them—in the garden and in the woods, singing and whooping, and all that stuff—could read and write English? Could they read and write? Oh, Lord, yes. Was First Baptist successful? Yes. Were First Baptist's daughter and granddaughter churches successful? Yes. And can you say the Bray School did not have something to do with that? I do not think you can.

Well, there you go. The tentacles of the Williamsburg Bray School are right there.

I would say another thing. If somebody asked me if I think the Bray School has affected me, I would say, "Yeah, of course it did." Think about some of the local Black schools. There was the James City County Training School. And we had Bruton Heights School. I wonder how many descendants of the Bray School students came through the Training School or Bruton Heights. I do not have a specific number, but they definitely came through.

There you have the tentacles of the Williamsburg Bray School. There they are, again.

The Honorable Robert "Bobby" A. Braxton is a native of Williamsburg, Virginia, who grew up on Braxton Court. He graduated from Hampton Institute (now Hampton University) and served in the United States Air Force. After a successful career as an engineer, Braxton returned to his hometown where he served on the Williamsburg City Council and where he continues to support local efforts including First Baptist Church's Let Freedom Ring Foundation and The Lemon Project at William & Mary.

Sir   Virginia Williamsburg 30th Sepr 1762

  Agreeable to your request we send you inclosed a list of the Negro Children now at the School under our Direction in this City, with an Account of their Ages as nearly as they can be judged of, but it is not in our Power to determine exactly the Dates of their Admission into the School, as various, some of them having been there ever since it was first opened & others admitted just as Vacancies have happened: the Mistress has not been so exact as to keep any Account of the Times of their Entrance; so that it is impossible for us to give the desired Satisfaction in this Point. You may from hence easily judge how difficult it must be for us to inform you particularly of the Progress each Child has made; We can only say in general that at a late Visitation of the School we were pretty much pleased with their Scholars Performance they rather exceeded our Expectations. The Children we believe, have all been regularly baptized; indeed we think it is a pretty general Practice all over Virginia for the Negro Parents to have their Children christened, where they live tolerably convenient to the Church or Minister; & some times a great Number of Adults are baptized together in different Parts of the Country. We would not have you think, from what was wrote you last Fall, that we had the least Inclination to discourage so good & pious an Institution; we were indeed & still are apprized of many Difficulties which we shall have to struggle with, & were therefore willing in some Measure to prepare you for a Disappointment, in Case the Undertaking should not answer your Expectations. From the small View we have had of the Associates extensive Charity, we flatter ourselves that we see the Situation of our poor Slaves, with Respect to their spiritual Concerns, with the same piteous Eyes that they do, & should think ourselves extremely fortunate, if any Endeavours of ours could contribute towards their Happiness. You no Doubt are already apprized that the Slaves in this & the neighbouring Colonies are the chief Instruments of Labour & we fear that they are treated by too many of their Owners as so many Beasts of Burthen; so little do they consider them as entitled to any of the Privileges of human Nature; & indeed many Owners of Slaves tho they may view them in a different Light & treat them with a great Degree of Tenderness, concern themselves very little or not at all with their Morals, much less do they trouble themselves with their religious Concerns; so far from it, that we don't think ourselves the least uncharitable in saying that we fear the Negroes are often corrupted & rendered more abandoned by the ill Examples which are set them by many white People in the Country, & no inconsiderable Number of these themselves Masters of Slaves. This Observation may be justified by a Comparison of new Negroes when they are first imported with those who have resided amongst us for some Years; for tho the former no Doubt bring with them vicious Inclinations & a Number of ill Customs, yet we may venture to say that they contract

TWO

1762: Exceeding Expectations

*Robert Carter Nicholas and Rev. William Yates
to Bray Associates, September 30, 1762*

Between Rev. John Waring's February 1760 appeal to establish a school for Black children and the first full report on operations at the Williamsburg Bray School in September 1762, both of the school's initial trustees, Thomas Dawson and William Hunter, passed away. Prior to his death in 1761, Hunter recommended William Yates and Robert Carter Nicholas as Bray School trustees, and both were approved by the Associates of Dr. Bray. Rev. William Yates succeeded Dawson as president of William & Mary and rector of Bruton Parish. Robert Carter Nicholas came from a very wealthy, slaveholding family in Virginia, and became treasurer for the colony of Virginia in 1766.

On September 30, 1762, Yates and Nicholas penned a letter to Waring which offered an account of "the Negro Children now at the School under our Direction in this City." The correspondence had three distinct parts: the trustees' narrative on operations and challenges facing the Bray School, an enclosed list of children then at school, and a list of regulations concerning the responsibilities of the teacher and the children's enslavers. The 1762 report indicated that the students "rather exceeded [their] Expectations." Three of the thirty students enrolled that September—Mary Ann, Mary Jones, and Elisha Jones—were free, and the overall ratio of boys to girls was essentially equal.

The 1762 student report is the only known record associated with the Williamsburg Bray School to offer ages for Bray School students who, at this time, were anywhere from three to ten years old. The ages of some free Black students were not recorded, which now denies us insight into their experiences at school and makes tracing their family histories more challenging. The Bray School rules were a product of editorial negotiation between Williamsburg and London, and emphasized instruction in reading, spelling, sewing, etiquette, and Anglican doctrines as much as the enslavers' obligations and the teacher's authority.

It is challenging to gauge the duration of Bray School students' attendance. Teacher Ann Wager, for example, had "not been so exact" in keeping record of their arrivals and departures. However, Yates and Nicholas did report that while some students entered as vacancies arose, other students had been there since the school's opening precisely two years earlier. The 1761 report on the school's opening did not include a student roster, so we do not know who, among these thirty students, were the first to matriculate.

While the letter, student list, and school rules do illuminate the early history of the Williamsburg Bray School, they do not directly share the perspectives of the scholars or their teacher. As the essays for this chapter make clear, it is important to consider the biases of the documents' authors as well as what voices have been silenced in these sources. It is critical to consider a range of experiences—both hidden and apparent—in the letter, school rules, and classroom regulations if we are to appreciate the nuanced and complicated history of the Williamsburg Bray School.

Letter Transcript
Robert Carter Nicholas and Rev. William Yates to Bray Associates

Virginia Williamsburg, 30th Sepr. 1762

Sir,

Agreeable to your Request, we send you inclosed a List of the Negro Children now at the School under our Direction in this City, with an Account of their Ages as nearly as they can be judged of; but it is not in our Power to determine exactly. The Dates of their Admission into the School are various, some of them having been there ever since it was first opened & others admitted just as Vacancies have happened. The Mistress has not been so exact as to keep any Account of the Times of their Entrance, so that it is impossible for us to give the desired Satisfaction in this Point. You may from here easily judge how difficult it must be for us to inform you particularly of the Progress each Child has made. We can only say in general that at a late Visitation of the School we were pretty much pleased with the Scholars' Performances, as they rather exceeded our Expectations. The Children, we believe, have all been regularly baptized; indeed we think it is a pretty general Practice all over Virginia for Negro Parents to have their Children christened, where they live tolerably convenient to the Church or Minister; & some Times a great Number of Adults are baptized together in different Parts of the Country. We would not have you think, from what was wrote to you last Fall, that we had the least Inclination to discourage so good & pious an Institution; we were indeed & still are apprised of many Difficulties, which we shall have to struggle with, & were willing to prepare you for a Disappointment, in Case the Undertaking should not answer your Expectations. From the small View we have had of the Associates' extensive Charity, we flatter ourselves that we see the Situation of our poor Slaves, with respect to their spiritual Concerns, with the same piteous Eyes that they do, & should think ourselves extremely fortunate if any Endeavours of ours could contribute towards their Happiness. You no Doubt are already apprised that the Slaves in this & the neighbouring Colonies are the chief Instruments of Labour & we fear that they are treated by too many of their Owners as so many Beasts of Burthen; so little do they consider them as entitled to any of the Privileges of human Nature; & indeed many Owners of Slaves, 'tho they may view them in a different Light & treat them with a great Degree of Tenderness, concern themselves very little or not at all with their Morals, much less do they trouble themselves with their religious Concerns, so far from it that we don't think ourselves the least uncharitable in saying that we fear the Negroes are often corrupted & rendered more abandoned by the ill Examples that are set them by many white People in the Country & no inconsiderable Number of these themselves Masters of Slaves. This Observation may be justified by a Comparison of new Negroes when they are first imported with those who have resided amongst us for some Years; for the the former, no Doubt, bring with them vicious Inclination & a number of ill Customs, yet we may venture to say that they contract new Vices, which they were Strangers to in their native Country. From this cursory View of the Situation of our Slaves, you may easily judge how extremely difficult it would be, if not morally impossible, to work any Thing like a thorough reformation amongst them, unless some of their Masters & the Generality of white People were first reformed, we had almost said new moulded. We would not have it infered from hence that we intend any particular pointed reflections upon the People of this Country; on the contrary we believe them as good to their Neighbours & think they are much of the same Complexion as the Inhabitants of other Countries. And 'tho we almost despair of an entire reformation, yet we have our Hopes that a Scheme ₍like₎

yours properly conducted, if it could meet with due Encouragement, might have a good Effect. We find that many People in this City, upon the first opening of your School, were well enough inclined towards it & if the Fund allotted was sufficient, we believe that double the Number of Scholars might easily be procured; but at the same Time we fear that many People who have sent or would send their little Negroes to School, would not do it upon the Principles which they ought; we mean purely with a View to have them instructed in the Principles of Religion & enabled to instruct their Fellow Slaves at Home. Some People we fear send their Children merely to keep them out of Mischief, others to improve them in Hopes, by their being made a little more sensible, that they may be more handy & useful in their Families; We form this Opinion from observing that several, who put their Negroes to School, have taken them Home again so soon as they began to read, but before ~~it~~ they had received any real Benefit or it could be supposed that they were made acquainted with the Principles of Christianity. This is one great Impediment which we are apprehensive will obstruct the Success of our Endeavours; We shall strive to guard against it, 'tho 'twill be with great Difficulty that we shall be able to accomplish our Purpose. Few People have more Negroes than they can employ & 'tho; when they are very young & useless, they may be willing to send them to School, yet when they grow up a little & become able to tend their Owners Children or do any other little Offices in their Families, they chuse & will take them Home. Another Difficulty which arises on the Part of the Owners is that an Opinion prevails amongst many of them, that it might be dangerous & impolitick to enlarge the understandings of the Negroes, as they would probably by this means become more impatient of their Slavery & at some future Day be more likely to rebel; they urge farther from Experience, that it is generally observable that the most sensible of our Slaves are the most wicked & ungovernable; these Observations, we think, are illy founded when used as Objections to your Schemes which we by no Means calculated to instruct the Slaves in dangerous Principles, but on the contrary has a probable & direct Tendency to reform Their Manners; & by making them good Christians they would necessarily become better Servants. We shall not fail endeavouring to remove Scruples of this & every other sort, but finding they have taken deep root in many minds, we are apprehensive of great Difficulties in overcoming them. There is still one greater Discouragement which we fear we shall labour under. Tho' the Owners of Negro Children should chearfully close with our Proposals & submit them entirely to our Government; 'tho the Mistress of the School should be ever so diligent in her Duty, & 'tho the Scholars should make as great a Progress as could be wished, yet we fear that, not withstanding all our Endeavours to prevent it; any good Impositions which may be made in the Children's Minds at School will be easily effaced by their mixing with other Slaves, who are mostly abandoned to every Kind of Wickedness. If evil Communications have a general Tendency to corrupt good Manners, the Observation is never more likely to be verified than in Instances of this Sort; where the very Parents of the Children will probably much of there, from their Intimacy set as bad an Example as others. Notwithstanding these & many other Difficulties, which the narrow Limits of a Letter will not permit us to particularize, stare us fully in the Face, we are resolved not to be discouraged; but hope, by the Blessing of God upon your Charity & our Endeavours, that the Undertaking will greatly prosper. The late Reverend M^r. Dawson & M^r. Hunter, we believe, had it in their Intention to form rules for the better Government of the School but were prevented by Death; we have hitherto contented ourselves with permiting the Mistress to carry on—the School in the way it was begun; but, being sensibile that nothing of the Sort can be properly conducted without certain uniform regulations, by which all Parties concerned may know how to govern themselves, we have drawn up such a set of rules as appear to us properly adapted & send you a Copy of them inclosed for your & the rest of the Associates' Approbation & should be glad to know your Sentiments; we shall be willing to add or diminish any Thing as you may advise. We probably shall have Occasion for a few Testament Psalters & spelling Books & perhaps a number of M^r. Bacon's Sermons, recommending the Instructions of Negroes in the Christian Faith, properly dispersed over the Country might have a good Influence. We would not put you to the Expence of any other Books at present. We will not conclude without offering our best respects to you & the rest of the worthy Associates; Believe us, Sir, we cannot enough admire a Set of Gentlemen, who at the same Time that they are employed in exercising every Act of Benevolence at Home, have so far enlarged their Charity as to extend it to the most distant Colonies.

We are, Sir, with the greatest Esteem

Y^r. most ob^t. hble Serv^{ts}.
Ro. C. Nicholas & Self
and M^r. Wm Yates

A List of Negro Children at the School established by the Associates of the late Reverend Doct[r]. Bray in the City of Williamsburg — M[rs]. Anne Wager — School Mistress

Names of the Children	their Age as nearly as can be judged of	Owners' Names
1 John	8 Years	M[rs]. Davenport
2 Anne	6	D[o.]
3 Dick	3	M[r]. George Davenport
4 London	7	M[rs]. Campbell
5 Aggy	6	D[o].
6 Shropshire	6	D[o].
7 Aberdeen	5	M[r]. Alex[r]. Craig
8 Mary	7	M[r]. Thomas Everard
9 Harry	5	D[o].
10 George	8	M[r]. Gilmer
11 Bristol	7	D[o].
12 Mary Anne	7	a free Negro
13 Aggy	7	Peyton Randolph Esq[r].
14 Roger	7	D[o].
15 Mary	8	M[r]. Thomas Hornsby
16 Rippon	3	M[r]. Anthony Hay
17 Robert	6	John Randolph Esq[r].
18 Lucy	5	D[o].
19 Elizabeth	10	M[rs.] Dawson
20 George	6	D[r]. James Carter
21 Locust	8	M[rs]. Armistead
22 Sarah	7	M[rs]. Page
23 Hannah	7	Ro: C. Nicholas
24 Mary Jones		a free Negro
25 John	7	John Blair Esq[r].
26 Jane	9	D[o].
27 Doll	7	D[o].
28 Elisha Jones		free
29 John	3	M[r]. Hugh Orr
30 Phoebe	3	M[r]. W[m]. Trebell

Wm[s]burg 30[th]. Sep[r]. 1762 1762

Rules & Regulations
for the better Government of the
Negroe School at Williamsburgh in Virginia.

The Associates of the late Reverend Doctor Bray, residing in England, having established Schools in several of the Northern Colonies for the Education of Negroes in the Principals of the Christian Religion teaching them to read & at the same Time rendering the Females more useful to their Owners by instructing them in sewing knitting & encouraged by the Success of these their pious Endeavours & being sollicitous to make this Kind of Charity as extensive as possible, they some Time ago came to a Resolution of establishing a School in the City of Williamsburg for the same Purpose I have thought fit to recommend it to the immediate Care & Government of The Reverend M^r. William Yates & M^r. Robert Carter Nicholas who have chearfully undertaken the Trust reposed in it & hope that all good Christians will cooperate with them in their Endeavours to promote the Success of so laudable & pious an Institution.

The Associates having engaged in so many Works of this Kind, which will require a very considerable Sum of Money to defray the Expence of, have limited the Number of Scholars to thirty; but as there may be many more Negro Children in their City equally Objects of such a Charity; The Trustees will thankfully accept of any Contributions which may be offered toward augmenting the Number & thereby rendering the Scheme more generally beneficial. If the Scholars should increase so as to make it necessary, they propose to employ another Mistress; And for the Satisfaction of their Benefactors they will be at all Times ready to give an account of their Proceedings.

The Trustees for the better Government of the School & to render it truly beneficial have thought fit to establish certain Regulations; relating as well to the Owners of Slaves as to the Teacher or Mistress; which they are resolved to have strictly observed & put in Execution, unless they should at any Time hereafter be induced by good Reasons to alter or relax them.

With Respect to the Owners

The School being at present full with the Number of Scholars proposed to be educated at the Expence of the Associates, such Masters or Mistresses who may incline hereafter to send their Negro Children to the School are desired to signify the same to the Trustees as they would choose hereafter that all Vacancies should be filled up by an equal Number from each Family as near as may be.

As it will be needless & by no Means answer the Design of the Institution for Children to be put to the School & taken away in a short Time before they have received any real Benefit from it, Every Owner before a Negro Child is admitted into the School must consent that such Child shall continue there for the Space of three Years at least, if the School should be so long continued.

A decent Appearance of the Scholars, especially when they go to Church, being very likely to make a favourable Impression; All Owners of Children sent to this School must take Care that they be properly cloathed & kept in a cleanly Manner; & if it should be agreeable, the Trustees ^{would} propose that the Children should wear one uniform Dress; by which they might be distinguished & it is conceived that this method would be attended within every little additional Expence.

The Owners must send their Negro Children regularly & constantly at the Hours of Schooling; must comply with all Orders relating to them & freely submit them to be chastised for their Faults without quarrelling or coming to School on such Occasions; must by no means encourage or wink at the Childrens Faults nor discourage the Teacher in the Performance of her Duty; But if there be any just Grounds of Complaint they must lay them before the Trustees & Acquiesce in their Determination, the Trustees engaging on their Part to act with the strictest Justice & Impartiality & that they will to the utmost of their Power endeavour to redress ^{every} just Grievance.

It is not doubted but that the Owners themselves will give the Children, when at Home, good Examples of a sober & religious Behaviour, but they must moreover take Care, as much as in them lies, that they are not corrupted by the wickedness or ill Examples of their Servants & other Slaves, must frequently catechize the Children at Home & second the Endeavours of the Teacher by inculcating in them the most useful & salutary Principles of Christianity.

Rules to be observed by the Teacher or Mistress, who is preferred to a Master as the Scholars will consist of Children of both Sexes.

1st She shall take no Scholars but what are approved ^{of} by the Trustees & She shall attend the School at seven O'Clock in the Winter half year & at six in the Summer half year in the Morning, & keep her Scholars diligently to their Business during the Hours of Schooling suffering none to be absent at any Time, but when they are sick or have some other reasonable Excuse.

2^{d}. She shall teach her Scholars the true Spelling of Words, make them mind their Stops & endeavour to bring them to pronounce & read distinctly.

3 She shall make it her principal Care to teach them to read the Bible, to instruct them in the Principles of the Christian Religion according to the Doctrines of the Church of England; shall explain the Church Catechism to them by some good Exposition, which, together with the Catechism, they shall publicly repeat in Church or else where, so often as the Trustees shall require & shall be frequently examined in School, as to their Improvements of every Sort.

4 She shall teach them those Doctrines & Principles of Religion which are in their Nature most useful in the Course of private Life, especially such as concern Faith & good Manners.

5 She shall conduct them from her School House, where they are all to be first assembled in a decent & orderly Manner to Church so often as divine Service is there performed, & before it begins & instruct & oblige them to behave in a proper Manner, kneeling or standing as the Rubrick directs & to join in the public Service

with & regularly to repeat after the Minister in all Places where the People are so directed & in such a manner as not to disturb the rest of the Congregation. She shall take Care that the Scholars, so soon as they are able to use them, do carry their Bibles & Prayer Books to Church with them; & that they may be prevented from spending the Lord's Day profanely or idly she shall give her Scholars some Task out of the most useful Parts of Scripture, to be learnt on each Lord's Day, according is their Capacities & shall require a strict Performance of it every Monday Morning.

6 She shall use proper Prayers in her School every morning & Evening & teach the Scholars to do the same at Home, devoutly on their Knees; and also teach them to say Grace before & after eating their Victuals, explaining to them the Design & Meaning of it.

7 She shall take particular Care of the Manners & Behaviour of her Scholars & by all proper Methods discourage Idleness & suppress the Beginnings of Vice; such as lying, cursing swearing, profaning the Lord's Day, obscene Discourse, stealing &c. putting them often in mind & obliging ₐ^them to get by Heart such Parts of the Holy Scriptures, where these Things are forbid & where Christians are commanded to be faithful & obedient to their Masters, to be diligent in their Business, & quiet & peaceable to all Men.

8 She shall teach the Female Scholars knitting, sewing & such other Things as may be useful to their Owners & she shall be particularly watchful that her Scholars between the School ₐ^Hours do not commit any Irregularities nor fall into any indecent Diversions

Lastly. She shall take Care that her Scholars keep themselves clean & neat in their Cloaths & that they in all Things set a good Example to other Negroes.

Remembering London

An essay by Janice Canaday

It seemed like just another fall day. The sun was shining, and the turning leaves were starting to fall from the trees. There was lots of chatter from students on a field trip here in Colonial Williamsburg's Historic Area. There were about thirty children in one particular group, so I walked over, stood to the back, leaned in, and listened. Students were told about Williamsburg as an eighteenth-century town: the people and their roles, status, and value. At the end of the conversation, students were invited to ask questions. I still watched and listened.

I soon saw that there were two African American ladies standing next to me—watching, listening, and asking questions. As I looked around the group, I realized that only one of the thirty students was African American. She did not ask any questions, so I asked the interpreter for permission to ask a question of the group. I wanted to know how they enjoyed seeing the town and learning the history of the folks that lived here. The African American girl smiled, but never spoke. It appeared she was forcing herself to smile—but it looked more like a grimace than a smile.

I asked the students what impressed them most about their tour and whether they had learned anything new. They answered, but the African American student said nothing. And so, I asked her if she had learned anything new. I asked her what her name was, and she told me it was London. As I proceeded with my conversation, she never really answered; she just shook her head and looked at the ground. I noticed tears welling up in her eyes, so I asked her if I had made her uncomfortable or if something in what I or the interpreter said had bothered her. She shook her head, no. Then I asked one last question: if the problem was with something that was not said. She nodded, yes. I walked over and asked to hug her, as tears dropped from her eyes. Still standing there, the two African American women told her that they understood and that it was all right.

In that moment, all of us were connected, not so much by what was said, but by what had not been said about us as African Americans. What was omitted was that in the late eighteenth century just over half of the town's population was Black, whether enslaved or free. So, there was nothing empowering or enlightening said to give London that "aha moment" that the other children had received. I said a few encouraging things to London, reassured her, and wished her well. As I walked back to my office, I thought about her name. *London*. I had seen that name before. That name was on a list of Williamsburg Bray School students. That London, who had attended the school in 1762, was about seven years old and belonged to tavern keeper Christiana Campbell.

I have to say that my encounter with London on a street in Williamsburg and my encounter with London in the Bray School records took my mind back to my days of schooling. When I attended school here in James City County, I certainly felt angst and uncertainty: unsure on one hand, but excited on the other. London here in the eighteenth century probably felt some apprehension, angst, and uncertainty attending the Bray School. For London on the Bray School list, was attending school something to look forward to or to dread? How did the students feel about the teacher, Ann Wager? Were Wager's words encouraging or dismissive? Did London feel seen and listened to when she (or he) attended the Bray School? Did she and her fellow students feel appreciated or just like property? Did the Williamsburg Bray School open a window of opportunity for the students to think and dream? Were London and the other children able to find their own voices? Did the school simply teach them how to stay in a place already laid out by those in power?

As African American interpretation at Colonial Williamsburg continues to evolve, these are the types of experiences, perspectives, and questions that must be addressed.

When I was in school, there was nothing said in my elementary years that made me feel empowered, enlightened, worthwhile, or capable. But someone did come along to speak words into my life that added light to my thinking. Who was that person for London at the Bray School and who will that person be for London who I met here? The Bray School seemed to take the students' individual voices and minds, and shape them to speak and think what enslavers wanted.

Education should help you to know that you are not restricted by someone else's dreams or vision for you. Oddly enough, I did not reach that conclusion about myself until I had six children of my own who I had to teach their self-worth and their capabilities.

I think about London from the Bray School and wonder if they ever knew this.

Janice Canaday is a lifelong resident of Williamsburg, Virginia, and a member of the Bray School Descendant Community. An educator and interpreter, she also serves as the African American Community Engagement Manager for The Colonial Williamsburg Foundation. "This is dedicated to my six sugarplums, Brittany, Devin, Adam, Ryan-Kristoff, Micah, and Maya. You all continue to fill my heart with joy each and every day; you inspire me to tell the stories that matter and to be kind—for that is true wisdom."

The Talented Tenth of Their Generation

An essay by Johnette Gordon-Weaver

On September 30, 1762, two trustees of the Williamsburg Bray School penned a letter to the Bray Associates in England. Robert Carter Nicholas and William Yates were the authors, providing updates on the local school for Black children. Nicholas and Yates were powerful men, and both were intent on the success of the Williamsburg Bray School. And while the goal of the Bray School was to indoctrinate Black children with religion and have them fully accept their station in life, I believe this was wishful thinking with virtually zero possibility of absolute success.

The more we learn, the more we want to learn, and the broader our perspectives become. At the same time, there is an air of surprise when Black students excel, regardless of the century. I am a product of this system. Being Black in Williamsburg during the civil rights movement, I felt the weight of having to work harder to be the best student I could. I am sure the Bray School Scholars felt the weight of these expectations as well. They were the Talented Tenth of their generation and were afforded an opportunity not given to everyone. These young scholars made a difference in Williamsburg, and their zeal for learning—and understanding its importance—is part of the tapestry of the community in which I was raised. My Nana, a product of the early 1900s, was famous for quipping "books before boys" and "pencils up, dresses down." Though she never acquired more than a fifth-grade education, she instilled in her family its importance.

As I perused the names of the children in the 1762 letter, they came to life for me. Their ages and names turned my focus to actual people, not simply figures of times gone by. I have looked over this list more times than I can count and with unexpected emotions. Many of the children lived along Palace Green. Many years ago, I was a seven-year-old child who played on the Green and daydreamed on the knoll behind the Everard House. Mary, a seven-year-old enslaved girl owned by Thomas Everard, was a Bray School student. What did she daydream about? When we look at the ages of these young people, we find that for some their formal education began early. Rippon, a mere three years old, was a Bray School student enslaved by Anthony Hay. Did Mary walk Rippon to school? Was that even allowed? What did the day look like for a three-year-old in such circumstances?

After waking early in the morning to walk to the Bray School, what greeting did they receive from their teacher, Ann Wager? Did they gather in groups to make their way to school while discussing the activities of the households where they were enslaved? My imagination leads me to believe that the happenings in the colonial capital gave them much to speculate and talk about. Hannah, another neighborhood student who was also seven years old, was enslaved by Robert Carter Nicholas himself. Did Mary and Hannah develop a friendship? We know that by the age of six or seven, these children had household responsibilities and duties, but was there ever time for giggles?

As a seven-year-old in 1960s Williamsburg, my responsibilities were my homework and keeping my room clean. I happily went off to school each day, eager to learn more and to show off for my parents each new word I learned to spell and how well I could read! My voracious appetite for reading allowed me to escape the doldrums of everyday life and visit faraway lands. Learning to read opens a world of possibilities, and surely none of this escaped our young scholars. Mary, Hannah, Aggy, and Lucy—they had to have imagined a better and brighter day for themselves as they gained knowledge. As much as I imagine what life was like in eighteenth-century Williamsburg for a Black child, it is difficult to do with a twenty-first-century mindset. What is not difficult to understand is that life in this community, this America, is filled with injustices.

As I stroll Colonial Williamsburg's Historic Area on early morning walks, I no longer walk alone. I carry Mary, Hannah, Lucy, Aggy, and Rippon with me. They walk with me, and they people the place I call home. They travel with me across the Atlantic and beyond. Because of them, I am. I live the spirit of Sankofa: I have gone back to fetch them and bring their humanity to us all.

Johnette Gordon-Weaver is a native of Williamsburg, Virginia, who traces her Hundley/Hunley and Roberts lines to the 1600s. Her fifth-great-grandfather, Anthony Roberts, served as a wagoner during the American Revolution. A proud alumna of Hampton Institute (now Hampton University), she is a former account executive for BSA Advertising. A community activist and advocate, Weaver is a member of the NAACP, The Village Initiative, Williamsburg Action, and Historic First Baptist Church. Her family is her pride and joy: her two sons are Hampton University alumni, her daughter is a graduate of the United States Naval Academy, and she has two grandsons and a granddaughter.

By Which They Might Be Distinguished

An essay by Tonia Cansler Merideth

The Williamsburg Bray School students hold many distinctions. They were likely some of the first Blacks formally educated in British North America. They were taught proper comportment and were expected to dress uniformly, to make a "favorable impression." It seems they did not disappoint. In his September 1762 letter of correspondence to the Bray Associates, Robert Carter Nicholas wrote that "at a late visitation of the School, we were pretty much pleased with the Scholars' Performances, as they rather exceeded our Expectations." This is truly remarkable given that the students faced harsh masters, unstable environments, and a curriculum that supported the ideology of slavery. They were brave little souls.

As Bray School Descendant Community members, we desperately want to know more about the lives of the Bray School students. We are not content to just know the names on a paper. Without other sources, however, we are left to imagine a day in the lives of the students. Rising early in the morning, I imagine they walked to school as many of us did as children. I see them entering the classroom, sitting down for their lessons, and being handed little primers and slate pencils. They studied words and recited passages. The girls were given needles to sew and knit. This is the scene I imagined in 2013 when I first saw the building that seven years later would be confirmed to be the Williamsburg Bray School.

I applied for graduate admission to William & Mary in 2018

but, unfortunately, declined acceptance. While writing the essay for this book chapter, I recalled that the admission application asked me to describe a living moment in history. I wrote about the day I saw and touched Prince George Street House, long rumored to be enveloping the Williamsburg Bray School. This is an excerpt of my submission:

> *When I reached out to touch the [building], I felt like I could hear [the students] laugh. I could see them looking at their teacher as she spoke, and I could hear her call them by name. This experience led me to research the history of education for African Americans and was one of my motivations for pursuing my degree in history.*

Ten years have passed since I first encountered the building on Prince George Street. I finished my master's degree at another institution, and in that time continued to visit Williamsburg and check on the progress of discovery. Thanks to the efforts of dedicated historians and researchers, that scene is now filled out more vividly for me. I have learned the names of many boys and girls who attended the school, the known history of the teacher, the location of the school, and the books they used in their lessons. I also learned that they were referred to as "scholars."

One of the Bray School Scholars on the 1762 list was named Locust, who was sent to the school by the Armistead family. Members of the Armistead family also owned my ancestors. Other enslaved persons owned by the Armistead family include James Armistead Lafayette, the Revolutionary War hero who contributed to the American victory at Yorktown by spying on the British. James was freed after the Marquis de Lafayette successfully petitioned on his behalf. James, in return, honored Lafayette by taking his name.

We do not know if Locust remained with the Armistead family, as no other records have yet been found that can help us with that determination. What remains are local oral histories that detail how some of the Bray School children returned to their communities and taught their families how to read and write even after it was illegal to do so. Eighteenth-century runaway ads contain the names of Bray School students who used their education to effect a change in their communities and to secure their psychological and physical freedoms.

As the oral historian for the William & Mary Bray School Lab, my hope is to connect with other Descendant Community members who may hold oral histories that can help us fill in the archival silences. Historical scholarship is not limited to traditional sources of gathering information about the past. Oral histories also hold valuable information we can use to learn more about our ancestors. We may be surprised to learn that the songs we sing, the stories we tell, and the traditions we follow are handed down from generation to generation. For persons of African descent, we carry our history within ourselves.

As a descendant, I want to use my voice to ensure that the story of the Williamsburg Bray School students becomes an American story. I want schoolchildren around the world to have the same vivid image of these distinguished scholars that I now have. Collectively, the Descendant Community will continue to add to the rich legacy left by the Bray School students, "by which they might be distinguished."

Tonia Cansler Merideth is the oral historian for the William & Mary Bray School Lab, Office of Strategic Cultural Partnerships, and a member of the Bray School Descendant Community. She credits her maternal grandmother, Ora Geneva Caldwell Ingram, with instilling in her a love of family. She dedicates her essay to Ora Geneva and her maternal great-grandmother, Malissa Armistead.

Rediscovering Roots and Rethinking Education

An essay by Leslie Gaston-Bird

I had given my mother a keepsake book when my son was born so that she could fill out our family tree. For some reason, she had not returned it to me; I just figured that she was busy. Shortly after my daughter was born a year-and-a-half later, Mom became ill. I went to her home and discovered the keepsake book had barely been filled out. She had written a name or two, but then stopped. Little did we know, Mom was developing dementia and could not remember her grandmother's name.

My mother's grandmother was Malissa (Armistead) Caldwell. My son and daughter are now eleven and twelve-and-a-half years old, and I still have the keepsake book Mom tried to finish. I am certain that Mom knew how important it was to tell stories of our family. When I was a young child, my mother recounted stories of her childhood to me: how she went to live with an aunt when she was a young woman; how her mother—Ora Geneva Caldwell, daughter of Malissa Armistead—started the first Girl Scout troop in her city; how she met my father. However, I did not understand the importance of the information that she passed along to me. I am grateful that my sister and cousins are taking an active role in recapturing that history, so that I can share it with my children in turn.

As I began writing my essay, I looked for the name "Locust," who was enslaved by the Armistead family. He belonged to the enslaver household of Jane Frances Anderson Armistead. The name "Frances" hit me like a bolt of lightning. Frances is my mother's name. All sorts of questions began to bubble up for me, the biggest of which were, "For whom was my mother named, and what was their legacy?"

Then, as I read the entries from the Williamsburg Bray School, I tried to imagine Locust (Armistead). Just eight years old—I remember when my kids were eight. How playful and active they were, and, of course, mischievous at times. But in those records, I came across a word I would not use to describe *any* child, and that word, "wicked," was recurrent in the correspondence from Robert Carter Nicholas and William Yates who described newly enslaved Africans as being prone to "wicked" tendencies. Imagine a child, traumatized from the crime of slavery, being treated with scorn, and labeled "wicked" and "incorrigible." We are not far from that world, of course, as we read stories of young Black children treated like criminals by their neighbors, even for merely being curious.

My career has been as an educator of young women and men at universities in the United States and England. I also started a separate program for women and underrepresented groups. As one of my peers reminded me, "When you educate a Black woman, you educate 10,000 people." I imagine that is what my grandmother, Geneva, embodied when she started the Girl Scout troop, or what my mother, Frances, imagined when she fought for women in her local AFL/CIO chapter, and as she worked for a charity that provided musical instruments for children in school. My calling to set up a program for underrepresented audio engineers was not an accident; I was taught to do this. Education is liberation. Or at least it should be.

In the case of the Bray School trustees, education was submission. What an odd conundrum. As Yates and Nicholas corresponded with the Bray Associates regarding the status of the school, it seemed to me there was a lot of "making the case"; of begging and pleading; of listing outcomes (the most important of which they considered to be obedience) for benefactors to consider.

Is education a tool for liberation or social control? Historical reflection would argue that it was easier in the 1760s to appeal to the interests of those looking to indoctrinate Black children than to empower the students. What, then, is freedom? Even today, efforts to educate marginalized populations depend on the goodwill and investment from those whose generosity can make or break our programs.

People often say, "Know your history." But perhaps it would be more powerful to emphasize the second word: "Know *your* history." I only wished I had been less passive when hearing my mother's stories. I have her fiery spirit and her fight. *From where did she get hers?* By sharing and preserving our stories, advocating for education, and working together, I am hopeful that we can build systems that empower us. But the warnings conveyed by the Williamsburg Bray School history seem clear to me: we cannot do it alone, and the goal must be to liberate.

Leslie Gaston-Bird, PhD, is a member of the Bray School Descendant Community. She is president of the Audio Engineering Society (AES) and a voting member of the Recording Academy (The Grammys®) who specializes in mixing sound for film. A senior lecturer at City, University of London, she is the author of Women in Audio *(Routledge) and* Math Fundamentals for Audio *(A-R Editions). A previously tenured associate professor of recording arts at the University of Colorado Denver, she is working on a project titled, "Immersive and Inclusive."*

The Legacy We Carry

An essay by Adam Canaday

As I sit and write this essay, I reflect on the time I have had to think about and struggle with the Williamsburg Bray School documents and with the school's history, both past and present. I think that it is important to read and acknowledge the existence of the Bray School documents, including the September 1762 letter and student list, but I think we need to refocus. And a good portion of focus should be on the children—the scholars—and their young minds. We have access to the full student list, so I will name only a few examples here. Aberdeen, Bristol, George, Locust, Rippon, Roger, Shropshire, and Elisha Jones. Anne, Aggy, Elizabeth, Lucy, Mary Anne, and Mary Jones.

    I am a member of the Bray School Descendant Community, the living blood of some of those children—children who took a seat at the table that was the Williamsburg Bray School, wondering if it was in their best interests. We now have an opportunity to stand up and not be seated at a table we did not set. We, in 2024, acknowledge that the chair at the table was never truly intended for our comfort; it was merely more convenient for those benefiting from a system whose rules they designed. *Some will say this does not sound like me or should not be in a book. But I say that it does, and it should.*

    My day-to-day struggle with history is with the question of which part of the truth people want. Not everyone wants to hear the same story and not everyone wants to hear the whole story. The struggle is with the interpretation and with whose interpretation we are talking about. What does the restoration of the

Williamsburg Bray School building mean for someone who does not understand the history and mission of the Bray Associates? The men who held the purse strings to fund the school and who held the pens to write these letters seem to carry much of the school's story hundreds of years later.

So, if we refocus on the Bray School students and their legacies across the Descendant Community, we see a broader, more complete story. When the names of the Bray School students are seen, it gives me joy to know that I can find my George Washington, my Thomas Jefferson, and our first ladies in the legacies of the Bray School. You can compare George Washington to the late Benjamin Lewis Spraggins who was the local NAACP president. You can compare Thomas Jefferson to the late Samuel Harris who owned the Triangle Block and the Cheap Store on Duke of Gloucester Street. And what about the Smith Brothers who founded and grew the successful Oleta Coach Lines? Our first ladies could be inspirational women like Mildred Walker and the late Clemenza Braxton.

The legacies of the Black children and families that were here in the eighteenth century remain centuries later. They are represented by places like Highland Park, Carver Gardens, Brookhaven, Ironbound, Roland Street, and Mooretown. These are local historically Black neighborhoods that are still predominantly Black. Those communities are the monuments to those who were here one hundred years ago. If you look at each neighborhood, they have somebody who has an ancestor in Williamsburg, York County, or James City County.

While the correspondence between the Bray Associates in London and the Bray School trustees in Williamsburg cannot tell the whole story, the documents serve an additional purpose. They can serve as a call to action. I want this story to be accessible to younger people in Williamsburg, both residents and visitors alike. If you are, say, thirty-five years or older, you are not likely to have a problem understanding the significance of the Bray School story. You are going to get it. But what about those who are under thirty-five? What about those who are under eighteen? How is this story speaking to them? Who is bridging the past and the present for them? I do not want them to be left out.

We all have a stake in this history. What are we, as a community, doing with it now? There lies in this moment the opportunity for each of us to find our call to action. Neither people nor institutions can change their pasts, but when they know better, they must do better. We must all do better. I end this essay by asking a question of reflection: What type of institution, community, or ancestor do we want to be?

I use the names of students like London, Bristol, Robert, and Phoebe as encouragement. Despite their circumstances and the inequitable structures that they had to navigate on a daily basis, they still moved forward. And so must I.

Adam Canaday is currently a coachman at Colonial Williamsburg. As a Bray School Descendant Community member and a local leader in movements for racial reconciliation and social justice, he dedicates this essay to his grandmother, Flossie; his mother, Janice—and all who have inspired him.

Williamsburg in Virga. 27th Decr. 1765.

Revd. Sir.

    I send you inclosed a List of the Negro Children who belong to the Charity School in this City. It is impossible for me to fix their Ages, but I suppose them to be from about four to ten Years; the Times of their Standing at School, from the Mistress's Acct. which she has not kept with any scrupulous exactness, are from about six Months to two or two & an half Years. The Rules which I formerly drew up for the better Gouvernment of this School & which you & the other Associates were pleased to approve, I would gladly have executed, but soon found that the Masters & Mistresses were so averse to every thing that lookt like Compulsion, that I thought it most adviseable to relax a little, in hopes that Things might be put upon a more agreeable Footing. You'll observe there are thirty four Children in the List, which exceeds the Number, which the Mistress engaged to teach; it is not in her Power to oblige them to give a constant Attendance & therefore, I believe, she is willing to instruct all such as offer themselves; The Owners of Negroes as soon as they are old enough to do little Offices about their Houses, either take them away entirely from the School, or keep them from it at Times, so that they only attend, when there is no Employment for them at Home. The Term which

THREE

1765: Patterns of Growth and Attrition

*Robert Carter Nicholas to Bray Associates,
December 27, 1765*

On December 27, 1765, Robert Carter Nicholas posted another letter and student list to the Associates of Dr. Bray in London. Due to the 1764 death of William Yates, Nicholas had become the school's sole trustee and the official voice of Williamsburg Bray School operations. The Williamsburg Bray School appeared to operate regularly despite personnel challenges and increasing political tensions in Virginia and throughout the British colonies.

While Ann Wager did not keep the attendance of her scholars "with any scrupulous Exactness," Nicholas believed that the matriculation of the average Williamsburg Bray School student lasted between six months and two-and-a-half years. Across the 1762 and 1765 school reports, we see the repetition of a few students' names, including Roger, who was enslaved in Peyton Randolph's household, and John, who was enslaved in the household of John Blair. Despite his best endorsements and attempts to lead by example, Nicholas admitted that enslavers removed students from the school once they were old enough to do "little Offices about their Houses." Enslavers kept children out of the Bray School entirely or allowed them to attend only when it did not compromise laboring interests in the colonial capital.

In the absence of consecutive teacher reports, we cannot gauge the consistency of attendance for any child, enslaved or free, nor can we determine whether there were any discernible differences in how long enslaved and free children attended the Bray School over time. What the December 1765 letter does reveal is that Ann Wager recorded thirty-four students in November, the highest number of students reported at the Williamsburg Bray School at any time between 1760 and 1774. Nicholas attributed this figure to Wager's willingness to teach "all such as offer themselves."

Worries about the toll that Wager's work was taking on her aging body did lead Nicholas to express apprehension about his ability to find a suitable replacement for her should she become infirm or even die. Additionally, high Williamsburg rents required Nicholas to consider another challenging Bray School scenario—relocating the school's operations to a more suitable building. Robert Carter Nicholas seemed resigned to his position, and he persevered as the Williamsburg Bray School's sole administrator, just as Ann Wager did as its only teacher. The school moved locations that winter, but its motivations and challenges remained largely unchanged.

Letter Transcript
Robert Carter Nicholas to Bray Associates

Williamsburg in Virg{a}. 27th Decr. 1765.

Revd. Sir,

I send you inclosed a List of the Negro Children who belong to the Charity School in this City. It is impossible for me to fix their Ages, but I suppose them to be from about four to ten Years; the Times of their Standing at School, from the Mistress's Acct. which she has not kept with any scrupulous Exactness, are from about six Months to two or two & an half years. The Rules which I formerly drew up for the better Government of this School & which you & the other Associates were pleased to approve, I would gladly have executed, but soon found that the Masters & Mistresses were so averse to every ^Thing that lookt like Compulsion, that I Thought it most advisable to relax a little, in hopes that Things might be put upon a more agreeable Footing. You'll observe there are thirty four Children in the List, which exceeds the Number, which the Mistress engaged to teach: it is not in her Power to oblige them to give a constant Attendance & Therefore, I believe, she is willing to instruct all such as offer themselves; The Owners of Negroes as soon as they are old enough to do little Offices about their Houses, either take them away entirely from the School, or keep them from it at Times, so that they only attend, when there is no employment for them at Home. The Term which I proposed for the Children to continue at School was Three years at least; few are allow'd to stay so long, but those, who do, generally learn to read pretty well & learn their Prayers & Catechism; tho' I fear that most of the good Principles, which they are taught at School are soon effaced, when they get Home by the bad Example set them there & for want of the Instructions necessary to confirm them in those Principles. I have a Negro Girl in my Family, who was taught at this School upward of three Years & made as good a Progress as most; but she turns out a sad Jade, notwithstanding all we can do to reform her. I am heartily glad to hear of the Success of your charitable Endeavours in the Northern Provinces; they have but few Negroes in those Places compared with the Number in Virginia & therefore I suppose they are not so much abandon'd. I have lately visited the school here & examin'd the Children, who seem to have made a reasonable Progress; the Mistress is pretty far advanced in years & I am afraid that the Business will soon be too laborious for her; & how to supply the school better I don't know. I am satisfied that she takes a great deal of Pains with the Children & I shall not fail to encourage her & do every Thing in my Power to promote the Success of so pious an Institution. I shall take the Liberty of making my annual Draught on you for £25 – payable to my Merch^t. M^r. John Norton. Wishing you & the rest of the worthy Associates a long Service of happy Years I remain very respectfully, Sir,

Y^r. most ob^t. hble Ser^t.
Ro. C. Nicholas

A List of Negro Children who are at the
Charity School in Williamsburg Novr. 1765

M^{rs}. Campbell's Young & Mary	2
M^{rs}. Davenport's William	1
M^r. Hay's Jenny	1
Doct^r. Carter's Nanny	1
M^r. Blair's John, Dolly, Elizabeth Catherine, Fanny, Isaac & Johanna }	7
M^{rs}. Burwell's Joseph & Davy	2
M^{rs}. Prentis's Molly	1
Col^o. Johnson's Squire	1
Col^o. Chiswell's Edmund & Johnny	2
M^r. Charlton's Nancy & Davy	2
M^{rs}. Grymes's Phillis	1
M^{rs}. Orr's Patt & Jack, James, & Sal	4
M^r. Thompson's Charles	1
M^r. Brown's Elizabeth	1
M^r. Thompson's Betty	1
Matt. Ashby's Harry & John	2
M^{rs}. Vobe's Sal	1
M^r. Waters's Sylvia	1
M^r. Randolph's Roger & Sam	2
in all	34

Clara, Johanna, Hannah, and Me

An essay by Hope Wright

History was always my favorite subject. I found it interesting to think about how people lived years ago. What would a young, Black girl like me be doing? Who would she become? I was always searching for myself in history. This was easy to find at home, where there were always books about Black history: African kings and queens, Black inventors, athletes, politicians. Growing up, *Ebony* and *Jet* magazines came to our house according to their respective monthly and weekly schedules. I saw Black girls—Black women—leading slave revolts, winning gold medals, and serving in Congress.

This was not the case, however, when it came to school. I rarely, if ever, heard about anyone Black in history or social studies. I looked for myself and who I could become in history, but did not find myself there. I attended Robert E. Lee elementary school. I remember as a young girl hearing a teacher talk about our school's namesake: He was a great general, he had a horse named "Traveler," he was respected. I remember coming home and talking about what we learned at school that day.

My older brother, who was a student at Hampton Institute, (now Hampton University) heard me talking about what we had learned about "the general," and he told me that my teacher had left out quite a bit. He told me that Robert E. Lee was fighting to protect a system that would have kept people who looked like us enslaved and legally classified as property, without any rights or freedoms. I felt let down. We did not learn about that part in school. I knew about history—Black history especially. I knew about slavery in this country and that the majority of people that looked like me had been enslaved. I understood this as a girl, but the Williamsburg Bray School really made me think about enslaved children as individuals who probably shared some of the same questions, opinions, and curiosities as I did.

I first learned about the Williamsburg Bray School when I was eight years old. The summer between third and fourth grade was when I began my decades-long career at Colonial Williamsburg. History was still my favorite subject. Knowing that this was an interest of mine, my mother took advantage of an opportunity presented to me later that year. I became a part of the first class of Junior Interpreters in the African American Interpretations and Presentations Department. This took a good bit of encouragement from my mother. I knew that I would have an opportunity to learn more about my history, but I was also expected to perform in a play in front of hundreds of people. This terrified me! But my mother, in her infinite wisdom, told me to take a chance—to see how things went and revisit this in a year. I ended up loving to perform. And one of the first historical figures I got to portray on stage was Elisha Jones, one of the Bray School students.

The students at the Williamsburg Bray School were names on a list, but they jumped off the page to me. I thought a lot about the children at the school. I knew the ages of some, and I knew their names in 1762, 1765, and 1769. I knew whether they were enslaved or free. If the children were not free, I knew who enslaved them. If they were free, I knew their parents' names. I thought about what the students were taught in the Bray School. I wondered if they had experiences like mine, where they were taught one thing in school and corrected at home by their family and community. I thought of Isaac Bee and his sisters, Clara and Johanna, parsing out what they learned with what was really true. I thought about how years later Isaac resisted his enslavement by running away from it. Twice! I thought about Hannah, who was described by her enslaver as "a sad Jade" and someone whom he wanted to reform. Maybe it was because she had questions about what she was learning; maybe she did not accept what was being taught to her.

I still think of the Williamsburg Bray School often. For years, the students' lives were not considered off the page. The focus was on the Bray Associates, the Church of England, the trustees, and even Benjamin Franklin. But the Bray School existed because of its students. They may have learned from pamphlets and texts, but they brought their curiosity, wonder, and intelligence with them to the classroom. They took the structured and narrow teachings that they received and questioned them, used them to help their families and communities, and resisted, in different ways, the injustices of the slave society into which they were born.

Hope Wright has worked at Colonial Williamsburg for nearly forty years in areas including performance, research, writing, and mentoring. She dedicates her essay to her loving mother, Marilyn Smith, who always encouraged and supported her.

Your Words Are Your Wand

An essay by Crystal Haskins

The December 27, 1765, letter from Robert Carter Nicholas, treasurer and administrator of the Williamsburg Bray School, to the London-based Anglican charity known as the Associates of Dr. Bray prompts me to reflect on my thoughts, intentions, and subsequent actions as a teacher, principal, and advocate for educational equity and justice. Florence Scovel Shinn wrote, "Our words are our wand," to emphasize the power of words as reflections of the hearts of men. I read this 1765 letter several times, trying to position myself and interpret the words as a Bray School student, as Ann Wager, as Robert Carter Nicholas, and even as a Bray Associate. I contemplated the many threads that tie together communities of learners and educators despite contrasts in ethics and time. I considered that this letter and the words used to be a wand that speaks to the complexity of eighteenth-century societal norms, human dynamics, and consequences.

During each read, my mind kept returning to Robert Carter Nicholas. I questioned the type of man he was in 1765, beyond a treasurer and administrator. What was his definition of humanity, and did he view these children as precious as the children he parented? Was he what Langston Hughes would describe as a "dream keeper" of the Bray children's heart melodies, or did he ignore the consequences of a dream deferred? Nicholas is the writer and holds this powerful wand; however, I questioned to what degree, if any, the voices of the students are represented or considered. This letter is more than correspondence from Virginia to England. It demonstrates the power of cause and effect, input and output, and the infinite power of our words. This letter is a stamp, a contract, and a verification of roles and responsibilities that propelled an ideology of control and ownership designed to dull the essence of Black children.

Yet, Robert Carter Nicholas and I are similar in some respects. We have contended with larger than ideal classroom sizes, changing student populations, and teacher shortages. I, too, have been faced with disagreement in our profession and, like Nicholas, thought "It most advisable to relax a little, in hopes that Things might be put upon a more agreeable Footing." We both have used words as magical wands to explain a condition, share what we believe to be true, and strategize to get what we want and believe are necessary. Despite our similarities, we have stark contrasts. I do not believe I have a rightful place to judge or cast an opinion on Nicholas because I do not know him outside of this text. Facilitating the learning of Black students has positioned us in common arenas, yet we embody different social priorities.

As an educator, a native of Williamsburg, and a student whose formative years were spent less than five miles away from the Bray School, I would be lying if I pretended that the colonized education demonstrated in 1765 had not embedded itself in my experience. It was noticeable in my actions and molded the way I see myself as a learner, educator, and an American. I wonder if Mrs. Orr's Pat, Jack, James, and Sal ever experienced the internal dialogues and conflict I did before going to school: *"Don't forget to talk like them. She don't know you like Momma and Daddy do. You ain't dumb. Show her."* Hence, my intonation would change. I practiced my subject-verb agreement and escaped my African American vernacular and other pieces of myself in order to blend into the education system. During that time, my words did not become my wand—I code switched and used a "wand" that seemed like the "right" one. I am in awe of the power of education and how its lingering residue can be palpable today. I am still working through my own exorcism from mindsets, policies, and curricula that intentionally or unintentionally framed many of my experiences, failures, and successes.

I cannot help but imagine the thoughts of the Bray School

children. Their bodies, souls, minds, and dreams were seemingly at the mercy of society's values in 1765. Was Elizabeth able to be Elizabeth? Did she pray and attend her catechism classes with excitement or confusion? Did this learning resonate with the spiritual knowledge passed down to her from her parents, grandparents, or fictive kin? Was she hopeful that the Bray School would cultivate her dreams, or did she know that her dreams could be deferred by Nicholas's pen?

This 1765 letter has survived through time and space to help us discover who we are as individuals and as a community. We are all educators and learners whose power is in recognizing and considering community by valuing each person and their truth—regardless of the similarities and contrasts to our own.

Crystal Haskins, PhD, is a native of Williamsburg, Virginia, who is constantly seeking ways to amplify her inner excellence and that of her family and community. She has served as a teacher and principal in the Williamsburg area and as the director of Equity, Assessment, and Strategic Operations for Newport News Public Schools. She is Chief Learning Officer for An Achievable Dream, Inc. A member of the Bray School Descendant Community, she dedicates this letter to those who seek to use their words and deeds for all, and seek to include those whose voices, words, and wands are still traveling to be asked about, heard, loved, and celebrated.

The Williamsburg Bray School: Conflict and Community

An essay by Burnell Irby

The Williamsburg Bray School operated from 1760 to 1774, and closed upon the death of its only instructor, Ann Wager. The school was in operation during a protracted period of unrest in the Americas that included the Seven Years' War, the subsequent road to the American Revolution, and slave resistance across the Americas. None of these events seemed to have greatly impacted the daily functions of the Bray School. Enslavement was entrenched in the surrounding counties of York and James City, and Williamsburg itself had a population that was more than fifty percent Black by the time of the American Revolution. This region had seen servitude evolve from a system of indenture to race-based chattel slavery. How did Williamsburg's Black community form under these circumstances, and how did the Bray School fit into this story? The Williamsburg Bray School documents are important to understanding this history because they describe the formation, operation, and enrollment at the school. The Bray schools comprised one of the oldest formal education systems for Black children in the thirteen British colonies. To be clear, Africans brought with them culture; many were skilled artisans and literate.

The Bray schools were not the only form of Black education in colonial America. Sources indicate that Black literacy was achieved through various means and that some William & Mary professors supported Black education prior to the founding of the Williamsburg Bray School. Nonetheless, it is incredible to imagine a functioning school for Black children operating within a system and region that over time would make literacy among enslaved Africans a crime. The documents included in this chapter have evolved over time into a voice for the voiceless; they describe the power relationship between the enslavers and the enslaved in colonial Williamsburg.

In the February 1760 letter, the intent of the school was stated as "Instruction of the Negro Children in the Principles of the Christian religion," a pious undertaking. Contrast it with a quote from the September 30, 1762, letter that describes the purpose of the Bray School, which states, "Another Difficulty which arises on the part of the owners is that opinion prevails amongst many of them that it might be dangerous and impolitic to enlarge the understanding of the Negroes, as they would probably by this means become more impatient of their slavery and at some further Date be more likely to rebel." Somewhere in between falls the information in Robert Carter Nicholas's December 1765 letter included in this chapter. The enrollment was at thirty-four scholars, but there were ongoing concerns about keeping track of students' ages as well as their time spent at school. Securing funding and supplies for the school was also a real concern. Nicholas described Ann Wager as willing and doing a good job, noting that the students who did stay learned to read and made "a reasonable Progress." Nicholas, in the 1765 letter, stated that the "Masters & Mistresses were so averse to every Thing that lookt like Compulsion," that scholars were removed from attendance at various points in their matriculation to return entirely to their forced labor.

The adults listed as the owners of the thirty-two enslaved students carried titles such as Mr., Mrs., Doctor, and Colonel. Matt Ashby was a free man of color who had two sons, John and Harry, attend the Bray School but was not afforded even a basic title. Where did Matt Ashby's agency come from to make Bray School enrollment happen in a school that focused on educating enslaved children? Having a record of Matt Ashby's full name also makes it easier to research his family beyond the Bray School documents. Indeed, there are Ashbys still living in the Williamsburg area.

The path to uncovering the lives of the other thirty-two children from the 1765 list is a tedious one that will require tracing them through documents of their enslavers; but developing a narrative is possible if one is willing to look beyond traditional eighteenth-century sources. Even so, this discussion of documents should center on the Bray School children. What was life like for them as enslaved people? What was it like for them as free children of color? How did they negotiate daily life in an environment that was inherently hostile to them as people of African descent? How do we begin to understand the impact of childhood trauma in the past, the present, and the future? Modern pedagogy is beginning to conceptualize Adverse Childhood Experiences (ACEs) as factors in how education is delivered. Williamsburg today continues to have a significant Black population, not unscathed, but intact through the legacies of the past.

Burnell Irby is a Howard University graduate, and an educator in Washington, D.C., and Maryland. As a youth, he spent his summers in Williamsburg at his great grandmother's home in Grove. He dedicates this essay to Carol, Louise, Cornelia, Cornie, Elizabeth, and Mary.

Exposure to Knowledge Is a Gateway to New Possibilities

An essay by Devin Canaday

I remember attending a conference on Educating Boys of Color. During an open discussion in a Science, Technology, Engineering, and Mathematics (STEM) education breakout session, one of the attendees shared his thoughts about STEM for our young men. He expounded on his disagreement with pushing Black boys into STEM, exclaiming, "Why would we want to have our boys in places where there is no one else that looks like them! We need to be getting them engaged in sports where they can excel, be around others like themselves, and improve their lifestyle." Being a professional engineer, consultant, and former collegiate athlete, I thought this was one of the most ignorant and shortsighted statements a person at an educators' conference could have made. All I could hear resonating in my head was, "All we are good for is dribbling, hitting, or kicking a ball."

Sadly, I see little difference in how the young Black children attending the Williamsburg Bray School had the value of their education viewed in comparison to the household functions and duties assigned to them by their enslavers. While I understand the times and station of the enslaved children, for me, it is still akin to denigrating what someone is passionate about as merely a waste of time. It is like dangling a savory treat before a hungry pup, then snatching it away the moment they catch a hold of it.

Consider the young girl referenced by Robert Carter Nicholas in his 1765 letter and how she became a "sad Jade." What made her sad? Could it have been her enslavement? Maybe it was due to her having to say goodbye to all her school friends. Or is it possible that her time at the Bray School gave her a sense of hope and excitement around learning, only to have the glimmer of hope torn away? We can only speculate. However, my experience working with young students from economically challenging and socially limiting backgrounds follows this same trend.

Initially, these young people believe themselves to be little more than the life circumstances from which they come. Yet, as they learn about the engineering design process and are provided opportunities to apply their newly acquired knowledge to solve real-world problems, their perspectives about life and their ability to affect the world around them shift drastically. Their exposure to knowledge becomes a gateway to new possibilities. If for some reason this gateway is locked, blocked, or vanishes, one may develop a sense of defeat. I imagine this is the same scenario that played out for the young students of the Bray School.

Still, one point that resonated with me from reading the 1765 letter was Ann Wager's willingness to take in every child offered to her. Despite the inconsistent attendance and uncertainty of a student returning from day to day, she was resolute in her efforts to educate every child. If one were to believe the creation and running of the Bray School comprised merely a social experiment, it is evident the schoolmistress did not get the memo. I have no doubt she was excited to see each child grow and learn, which likely fueled the students' motivations to rise to the occasion. Alongside their sense of purpose sourced from their learning, her encouragement engendered confidence in the children.

So, it stands to reason that Robert Carter Nicholas's assertion about the success achieved in the Northern Provinces was a valid one. If these students were "not so much abandon'd," then it was reasonable to expect that they would continue on an upward learning trajectory. Those closest to the work, Wager and Nicholas, expressed their support for "so pious an Institution." The reality is that several enslavers saw little value in this form of education. To most of them, the school was a frivolous philanthropic endeavor that would bear little fruit. And what fruit it did bear would likely not be worth the pluck.

The social exercise of propagating the belief in young Black children's limited capacity to learn and excel still lingers to this day. When asked if there are Black engineers, scientists, and mathematicians, students quickly respond with "no" or "not that many." Many Black students do not see themselves in these spaces, and some even believe they do not belong. The work of dispelling these myths about our ability to achieve scholastic heights is one of grave importance. It has roots that incorporate institutions like the Williamsburg Bray School. The legacy of the work by people like Ann Wager, with support from advocates like Robert Carter Nicholas (regardless of the true motivations), must continue in order that we might continue our "reasonable Progress."

Devin Canaday is a member of the Bray School Descendant Community who takes pride in his experience working at Colonial Williamsburg. The opportunity to help tell this story served as a foundation and launch pad for his career in engineering. Today, he continues employing these roots as a STEM Consultant—training teachers and exposing students to the potential of careers in STEM fields.

Unfinished Business: The Williamsburg Bray School Experiment

An essay by Vicki Anderson Simons

It is often said that America is an experiment. If that is true, African Americans figure prominently within our national laboratory. I believe that, as a people, African Americans have been tested on so many fronts based on perceived mental, physical, and emotional capabilities, and have endured the breadth of race-based opinions and policies about who we are, where we should be, what we do, and our value in American society.

The story of the Williamsburg Bray School offers an intriguing starting point for assessing the benefits of early education for enslaved and free Blacks. The school was founded in 1760, when Virginia was a British colony and before America declared its autonomy in the Declaration of Independence in 1776. Slavery was already well established, and the contributions of enslaved Blacks were an integral part of Virginia's economic success. The school's exact objectives are paradoxical. The Bray Associates acknowledged the humanity of Black people, but supported a society that enslaved them. Oddly, the school also enrolled free Blacks although not much is known about them. In addition, many white enslavers viewed Blacks as subhuman and deemed the school unnecessary and dangerous. This juxtaposition—the advantages and disadvantages of educating Blacks—points to the ongoing debate among some white colonists as they moved away from the British crown toward a caste system of their own.

In December 1765, Nicholas penned a letter to the Bray

Associates voicing his concerns about the scholars and the future of the school. He complained that students were not consistently enrolled for the recommended three-year period and was apprehensive about bad influences from newly imported Africans, and enslavers who prioritized home duties over formal education. Ironically, Nicholas optimistically reported students were making progress despite these challenges.

If I were to reluctantly take slavery out of the picture, these concerns might appear noble. Nicholas recognized the students' humanity and advocated for their uninterrupted tenure at the school. This notion runs counter to the contemporaneous sentiment of some enslavers, as highlighted in Nicholas's 1762 letter, which stated that the Bray School Scholars were "treated by too many Owners as so many Beasts of Bur[den]; so little do they consider them as entitled to any of the Privileges of human Nature."

We know what the school's *founders* believed, but what of the Bray *Scholars*? They are the silent objects of this educational experiment. In some cases, they would have been more educated than whites who could not afford a formal education. In 1765, there were thirty-four scholars, approximately three to ten years of age. Their typical school day started at 7 a.m. in the winter and 6 a.m. in the summer. What would they have been thinking and feeling? I shudder to think about it. Consider Phoebe, a three-year-old girl listed on the 1762 school roster. She likely rose before dawn, attended to matters required by her enslaver, and readied herself for school. She was taught to read, spell, recite catechism, sew, and knit, in accordance with her age. Despite being in the lowest part of the colonial caste system, this three-year-old served as a model of the Bray Associates' precepts and was expected to blossom into obedience and usefulness with no agency of her own.

My modern mind wants to know how the Bray School experience impacted its child scholars like Phoebe in 1762 or Squire in 1765. Did they feel blessed, cursed, or both? If we draw from the documented experiences of enslaved people who learned to read and write English, we know that education was a risky proposition, strongly discouraged within white society and later punishable by death. Education may have activated imagined possibilities that did not align with realities of enslavement or ignited discontent leading to disobedience, resistance, and potential harm. How did these young children navigate a society where they were socially on the bottom rung, but still educated? Were they able to utilize their education to become free?

For now, many of these questions remain unanswered. My hope is that the William & Mary Bray School Lab finds and reveals the hidden stories and experiences of the Bray Scholars, enslaved and free. Their experiences, which go well beyond a restored school building, are part of the epilogue of the African American experience and American history. Without knowing more about the students' lives, the success or failure of the Bray School experiment will forever remain inconclusive.

As I allow myself to speak with a modern mind, I wish to tell this to the Bray School Scholars:

Your experience is our model of inspiration. We celebrate you. We survived slavery, Reconstruction, Jim Crow, and more. We are educated and valuable contributors in every aspect of American society. We will never forget you.

Vicki Anderson Simons, Esq., is an attorney, historian, and civil rights advocate who served as the national director of the EPA's Office of Civil Rights. For more than thirty years, she has dedicated herself to unveiling hidden stories of her ancestors and others who share similar experiences in York County, Virginia. She is a founding member of the Hundley History Committee, and Friends of the Reservation Charles Corner, a descendant-community organization in Williamsburg, Virginia. Simons holds a Bachelor of Arts in Public Relations from Howard University, and a Juris Doctor from the University of Maryland School of Law.

Revd. Sir.   Williamsburg in Virga. 16th February
                                                            1769.

  I have received both your late Letters & am sorry to find you expressing the least Dissatisfaction at my Conduct with Respect to the Negro School in this City, the Success of which I have done every Thing in my Power to promote. When I first engaged in this Business, tho' I could not but very cordially commend the pious Designs of its Authors, yet I was aware of the many Difficulties it might meet with & therefore communicated them to you freely & without Reserve. I formerly sent you a List of the Negro Children at School & could only in general observe that I thought they were properly attended to & had made as good a Progress as I expected, all things consider'd. I don't know what farther Information I can give; the Children are so often shifted, that it would be almost endless to attempt giving you the Dates of their Entries, & Times of leaving the School. The Regulations which I formerly drew up & transmitted to you, I was in hopes of carrying into Execution, but have been disappointed in several Respects. I send you a List of the Children now at School & another of those who have left it. The Books you sent I have taken Care of; the Mistress has such as she wants from Time, & I have occasionally lent & given others of them to grown Negroes in different Parts, who I thought would make a good use of them; this measure I consider'd as cooperating with your principal Design, & hope you will approve of it. It gives me Pain that you should suppose I had exceeded your Limits so far as you mention. You may Remember that I succeeded Mr. Hunter in this Business & of Course must have conform'd to your Directions to him, when not altered by subsequent Instructions to me. Give me leave to quote a Passage or two from yr. Letter to him of the 1st. of June 1761. viz; "They (meaning the Associates) acknowledge that they "are not competent Judges what Salary may be sufficient "for a Mistress & therefore must refer that Matter entirely "to your Prudence & Discretion, but as they paid no more "than £20 Stg. for 30 Children both at Philadelphia & "New York City, they hoped the same Stipend might be "sufficient with you, however that this Undertaking may "meet with no Check or Discouragement in its Infancy,

FOUR

1769: An Increasingly Fractured Relationship

*Robert Carter Nicholas to Bray Associates,
February 16, 1769*

As political and social tensions continued to mount across the British Empire, the correspondence from Williamsburg to the Bray Associates also reflected the strained relationship between imperial and colonial metropoles. Now the sole Bray School trustee, Robert Carter Nicholas expressed both his distress and frustrations in continuing the operations of the Williamsburg Bray School. In his letter to the Bray Associates dated February 16, 1769, Nicholas articulated a litany of complaints and concerns, reflecting a moment of rather intense standoff between himself and the Bray Associates.

The tone of Robert Carter Nicholas's 1769 letter was set from the very beginning as he shared his regrets that the Bray Associates had expressed "the least Dissatisfaction at my Conduct with Respect to the Negro School in this City, the Success of which I have done every Thing in my Power to promote." As the longest-serving and the most prolific writer of all the local trustees, Nicholas had, indeed, become locally and internationally synonymous with the continuation of the Williamsburg Bray School.

Harsh tones aside, this letter serves as a brief primer on the history of Bray School administration in Williamsburg and of transatlantic communications between Williamsburg and London. The subject of Bray School finances runs deep throughout the letter and is a key sticking point, as is the case with several different pieces of correspondence associated with this school. Robert Carter Nicholas frequently put Rev. John Waring, the Associates' secretary, in remembrance of when and how money had been spent to support the Bray School enterprise. This remembrance primarily centered upon paying Ann Wager an adequate salary and securing rent on a building of sufficient size amid the clearly volatile rates of exchange between British and Virginian currency.

In his letter, Nicholas also expressed frustration over enslavers' failure to keep students in school for the recommended length of time, as well as a pattern of students being shifted into and out of regular attendance. Nicholas informed Waring that he was including two enclosures with the letter: "a List of the Children now at School & another of those who have left it." We have access to the first of the two referenced documents, a list of thirty student attendees—twenty-eight enslaved and two free. However, the list of students no longer at school has not yet been found among Bray Associates' records and may have not survived.

What about the students? Based on the letter and student list sent to the Associates of Dr. Bray that February, it is unknown how students felt or what they experienced at the Williamsburg Bray School. Regardless, we do know the thirty names of the children who attended the Bray School during the winter of 1769. While we may not know their opinions or feelings from this correspondence, it is imperative that we consider the lasting impacts of this instruction on the Black Williamsburg community at a time of increased political strain and protest of British taxation.

Letter Transcript
Robert Carter Nicholas to Bray Associates

Williamburgh Virg^a. 16th. February 1769.

Rev^d. Sir

I have received both your late Letters & am sorry to find you expressing the least Dissatisfaction at any Conduct with Respect to the Negro School in this City, the Success of which I have done every Thing in my Power to promote. When I first engaged in this Business, Tho' I could not but very cordially commend the pious Designs of its Authors, yet I was aware of the many Difficulties it might meet with & therefore communicated them to you firmly & without Reserve. I formerly sent you a List of the Negro Children at School & could only in general observe them I thought they were properly attended to & had made as good a Progress as I expected, all Things consider'd. I don't know what farther Information I can give; the Children are so often shifted, That it would be almost endless to attempt giving you the Dates of their Entries & Times of leaving the School. The Regulations which I formerly drew up & transmitted to you I was in hopes of carrying into Execution, but have been disappointed in several Respects. I send you a List of the Children now at School & another of those who have left it. The Books you sent I have taken Care of; the Mistress has such as she wants from Time, ^[illegible] & I have occasionally lent & given others of them to grown Negroes in different Parts, who I thought would make a good Use of them; This measure I consider'd as cooperating with your principal Design,

& hope you will approve of it. It gives me Pain that you should suppose I had exceeded your Limits so far as you mention. You may Remember that I succeeded M^r. Hunter on this Business & of Course must have conform'd to your Directions to him, when not alter'd by subsequent Instructions to me. Give me Leave to quote a Passage or two from Y^r. Letter to him of the 1st. of June 1761. viz; "They (meaning the Associates) acknowledge that they are not competent Judges what Salary may be sufficient for a Mistress & therefore must confer that matter actively to your Prudence & Discretion, but as they paid no more than £20 st.^{g} for 30 Children both at Philadelphia & New York City, they hoped the same Stipend might be sufficient with you, however, that this Undertaking may meet with no Check or Discouragement in its Infancy on this Account, they have directed me to acquaint you that they cheerfully increase their Appointment to £30 st.^{g} not doubling, but in Time a Proposal for a Subscription towards its Support will be favourably received at Williamsburg in the meanwhile they would "be glad the Number of Scholars were increased to 30 agreeable to their first Proposal & to the Number instructed in their other Schools &.^{c}" The Number of Scholars was at first, as I understood, only 24; this Letter coming to my Hands, soon after M^r. Hunter's Death I had the Number increased to 30 & obliged the Mistress, that there might be no partiality shown to white Scholars of which she then had about a dozen, to discharge them all & this at the Risque of the Displeasure of their Parents, with whom she was in high Repute for her Care & Method of teaching. Having this Letter for my guide & Direction, you may easily Judge at my Surprize to find you complaining that I had advanced the Salary to £25 st.^{g} without proper Authority, M^r. Hunter had fix'd the Mistress's Salary at £7 a Quarter, a Sum, for 30 Scholars, much less than is paid for Schooling in this City to other Mistresses; but, as M^{rs}. Wager ~~was~~ had no House of her own, she was at first allow'd £8 curr^t. Money more to pay for the Rent of a House, which was much too small for such a Number of Children; however she continued in it, as long as it was tenantable; I was then obliged to rent the House, where she now resides, of M^r. President Blair, for twelve Pounds curr^t. Money. My first Bills were only for £25 st.^{g}; this did pretty well with my advancing, generally, a Y^r. Salary before I drew the

Bills & when our Exchange was at 55, 60, 60 & 40 PC^t. but, when Exchange fell to 25 PC^t.; you see that £30 st.^{g} yielded not enough to pay the Salary & Rents; if you'll be pleased to calculate, you will find that my Draughts upon an Average are considerably under £30 st.^{g} besides that I have generally been considerably in Advance, a Circumstance, which I never regarded & should not mention it, but upon this Occasion. As to raising Money by Subscription, I have sounded many of the Inhabitants, but never had the least Encouragement to hope for success in such a Scheme. I have still ventured to continue the School upon the old Footing till I know the Associates farther Pleasure, after they have been made thoroughly acquainted with the whole Matter & reconsider'd it. I have my hopes that they will think there is some Consideration due to the Mistress, who has actually thrown herself out of other Business by engaging in theirs. I could not at any Rate discontinue any Part of the Allowance before the first of January last, as both she & her House were engaged for the year certain. I think, that I before sent you my Acc^t. to Decr. 1766, when I drew for £37.10 ^{stg} the exact Bal^{ce}. then due to me; I send you now my further Acc^t. by which it will appear that then is now due to me £42.10 Curr^t. Money, for which I have drawn on you to my Friend M^r. Norton, & can have no doubt of its meeting with due Hon^r. If there should be any Mistake in the Account, it shall be immediately rectified upon being pointed out. You have forgot another Thing, I mean the Death of my very worthy Friend the Rev^d. M^r. Yates, who left us several Years ago, of which I [page torn] soon after advised you. I am very respec[tfully Rev]^d. Sir,

                                            Y^r. Mo. Ob^t. Servt.
                                            R.C. Nicolas

Negroes now at School.

M^rs^. Prisc.^a^ Dawson's Grace	1
M^r^. R.C. Nicholas's Sarah.	1
M^r^. Presid^t^. Blair's Cath^ne^., Nancy, Jan^a.^ & Clara Bee	4
M^r^. Hay's Jerry, Joseph, Dick	3
M^rs^. Chiswell's Jack.	1
M^rs^. Campbell's Mary, Sally, Sukey	3
M^rs^. Speaker's Sam	1
M^rs^. Vobe's Jack.	1
John & Mary Ashby … free	2
M^r^. Ayscough's Sally.	1
The College. Adam, Fañy	2
The Commissary's Charlotte	1
M^rs^. Blaikley's Jenny, Jack.	2
Hon. Robt. Carter's Dennis.	1
M^r^. Hornsby's Nancy, Judy, Ratchel.	3
M^r^. Cocke's Mourning	1
M^r^. Davenport's Matt, Harry.	2

A Bray School Descendant

An essay by Theodora "Teddi" Ashby

The Williamsburg Bray School opened on September 29, 1760, with a charge from an Anglican philanthropic organization composed of upper class, educated, and monied white men to focus on converting perceived non-Christians—specifically Native Americans and enslaved and free Blacks—to the Anglican faith and membership in the Church of England.

My Bray School letter is dated February 16, 1769, and is written by Robert Carter Nicholas in correspondence with Rev. John Waring of the Bray Associates in London. Nicholas was related to Carter Burwell, who owned Virginia's famed Carter's Grove plantation. The Ashbys have a connection to Carter's Grove. In my great-uncle William Mobile Ashby's book, *Tales Without Hate*, it states that his grandfather, William S. Ashby (1820–?), inherited approximately thirty acres of land in a settlement called Carter's Grove, along the James River in James City County. It is said that all Blacks who lived in that community were free.

My Ashby family descends from an English woman named Mary Ashby and an African man whose name is yet unknown. Mary Ashby was indentured to James Shields, owner of Shields Tavern, and had three children: Matthew (ca. 1723), John (ca. 1725), and Roseanna (ca. 1732). Because Mary Ashby was free, her children were free. However, because Mary Ashby crossed the color line by having children with a man of African descent, she was required to pay a fine for the birth of each child. Their son, Matthew, wanted more for his family and worked as a carter, blacksmith, and a carpenter to earn money. He negotiated with Samuel Spur the terms and conditions to purchase his wife, Ann, and his children, John and Mary, for £150. To ensure his children would be free, Matthew Ashby then petitioned the court for their freedom.

I am a descendant of three known Williamsburg Bray School Scholars—Harry, John, and Mary Ashby—the children of Matthew and Ann Ashby. In February 1769, Robert Carter Nicholas reported "John & Mary Ashby... free" as among the children "now at school," based on the student list provided by Ann Wager. Four years prior, in his 1765 report, Nicholas noted "Matt Ashby's Harry & John" as attending the Bray School. Given the four years that elapsed between these two dates, it is quite exceptional to find John Ashby's name on both the 1765 and 1769 student lists. This could easily lead to the conclusion that John Ashby attended the Bray School uninterrupted from 1765 to 1769, but this is impossible to say without more information about the intervening years.

The Ashby children's free status meant their attendance at the Williamsburg Bray School did not come with the same apprehensions or suspicions about being educated as did the enslaved children. Robert Carter Nicholas desired to have children attend the Bray School for at least three years, and the enslavers' opposition to this length of schooling as outlined in his letter seemed not to apply to the Ashby family. Matthew Ashby, a free man of color, knew the value of literacy and may have ensured that his children attended the Bray School for as long as possible. The inventory of Matthew Ashby's estate shows that the family had a home in Williamsburg with supplies, furniture, and books. Each person had their own bed and linens. The list of supplies indicates that Ann may have worked as a laundress. Matthew Ashby died on April 15, 1771, in Williamsburg.

My great-grandmother, Sarah Gary Ashby (1851–1913), declared how important education was to her family in response to my great-grandfather, William "Button" Ashby (1843–1900) suggesting they move to the country. "I ain't going to do it. I ain't going to take my children back in them woods where they can't get no schooling!" I heard from my father, Aubrey C. Ashby, many, many times that the Ashbys were always free people and educated. I have also repeated this fact to my children, Sterling and Phillipa Ashby.

The annual Ashby Family Reunion was first held in 1968 at Egg Harbor Lake, New Jersey. Our Great-Uncle Bill (1889–1991) and Aunt Mary (1894–1988) attended. Uncle Bill recounted our family history and showed us the manumission document when Matthew Ashby freed his wife and children. This is where I learned that our ancestors attended school during the colonial period. We continue to make Ashby family history the focal point of the reunion, and in 2023, I was stationed at the site of the Williamsburg Bray School to engage with family and answer questions. The annual reunion's importance lies in reinforcing and expanding the true Ashby history—in which Matthew Ashby purchased Ann and his children and then petitioned for their freedom—as a source of inspiration and motivation to each generation in the twenty-first century.

Theodora "Teddi" Ashby has been a family history researcher for more than forty years, prompted by her son Sterling's homework assignment to complete a three-generation family tree. She is a member and twice president of the African American Genealogy Group of Philadelphia. A long-serving member of St. Mary's Episcopal Church in Ardmore, Pennsylvania, and the Overbrook Park Civil Association, Teddi Ashby is a Pennsylvania-licensed Realtor, and a member of both the National Association of Realtors (NAR) and the National Association of Real Estate Brokers (NAREB). She writes this essay in memory of Sterling Todd Ashby, her "reason to know more."

A Tale of Two Points of View

An essay by Jody Lynn Allen

I grew up in Hampton, Virginia, approximately thirty minutes southeast of Williamsburg, and visited the town on school field trips. While I remember few details about those experiences, I clearly learned, by their absence in the reconstructed colonial town, that there were no Black people in eighteenth-century Williamsburg. I was a graduate student at William & Mary before I learned the truth—that there was a Black majority around the time of the American Revolution. There are three possible reasons why the Foundation chose to tell only part of the story. First, they believed that the Black presence was tangential to the history of Williamsburg. Second, they feared that acknowledging Black people meant acknowledging their status as enslaved, a story that might reflect negatively on the white inhabitants of the time and those living in the twentieth century. Third, researchers failed to read the available texts closely, thus missing vital information.

Today, we know a good deal about slavery in North America, and while uncovering the voice of the enslaved is still a challenge, if we pay attention, we can find them through what the enslaver said and what they leave out. In short, we are engaging with the archive in ways that are opening doors thought forever closed. Black people are no longer accepting the notion that it is impossible to know their history, and scholars are asking new questions of the archives and uncovering untold stories through the technique of close reading.

The letter addressed in this essay, written by Robert Carter

Nicholas in February 1769, is but one example of the reconsideration of an historical source found long ago and now being reviewed for what it can tell twenty-first-century readers. Here, Nicholas responded to a letter from Rev. John Waring of the Bray Associates. In it he shed light on enslavers who sent enslaved children to the Bray School. The letter tells us that not all enslavers were comfortable with the idea of educating Black children, and sometimes withdrew the scholars from the school before they completed the prescribed course of study. This action confirms that the enslaved lived at the whim of the enslaver who perhaps felt threatened, even fearful of Black people who could read. Indeed, reading was a source of power.

We also learn that the institution of slavery varied from one enslaver to the next. Nicholas did not fear learned enslaved people. He supported their finishing the complete, three-year course of study, and he made sure that Ann Wager received the books provided. Even more interesting, he "occasionally lent & [gave] other of them [books] to grown Negroes in different Parts, who [he] thought would make good use of them."

Nicholas also shed light on his opinion of the children's capability when he wrote that they "had made as good a Progress as I expected, all Things consider'd." Did he have low expectations for the children's success? Was he referring to their social status or the negative feelings of some enslavers toward the school? Perhaps he believed that Black children were less educable than white children. Of course, this lack of confidence in their intellectual abilities allowed Black people to operate under the radar for their own benefit and the benefit of others. For example, the school was nine years old when Nicholas wrote the letter. Bray School attendees or graduates likely taught others in their community to read the books that Nicholas mentioned loaning out.

Additionally, Nicholas forwarded to the Bray Associates a list of the thirty children attending the school at the time—twenty-eight enslaved and two free. The list includes names, which makes it invaluable. Indeed, the names of enslaved people are often missing in favor of descriptions like "Carter's girl" or "Braxton's boy." This list also confirms that in addition to wealthy white men, there were clergy, white women, institutions like William

& Mary, and signers of the Declaration of Independence who enslaved people. Finally, by naming the students, Nicholas, whether intentionally or not, acknowledged their humanity and provided a useful resource for historians, genealogists, and descendants working to uncover Black life in colonial Virginia more than two centuries later.

At one point in time, Robert Carter Nicholas's 1769 letter to Rev. Waring told the reader only about Nicholas and his white contemporaries. Today, with the benefit of fresh eyes, it tells us about enslaved Black people who lived challenging yet meaningful lives. They lived in a time when restrictions tightened, but also when learning to read was a possibility. It was a time when Black people held and exercised a modicum of power that some white people recognized and were forced to respond to. Today, some people interpret the existence of the Williamsburg Bray School as proof that slavery was not so bad. In reality, this was a time before it became illegal for Black people of any age, enslaved or free, to read. It was a time of possibilities.

Jody Lynn Allen, PhD, is an assistant professor of history and the Robert Francis Engs Director of The Lemon Project at William & Mary. Her research interests cover the broad span of African American history focusing on Black agency and resilience.

London. Feb: 29: 1760

Rev'd Sir

I am desired by a Society who call themselves The Associates of the late Dr. Bray (the Objects of whose attention are the Conversion of the Negroes in the British Plantations, founding Parochial Libraries & other good purposes) to acquaint You that lately agreed to open a School at Williamsburg in Virginia for the Instruction of Negro Children in the Principles of the Christian Religion. They earnestly request that You Mr. Hunter, Postmaster & the Minister of the Parish will be so kind as to assist them in the Prosecution of this pious Undertaking; that You will with all convenient Speed open a School for this purpose: & as 'tis probable that some of each Sex may be sent for Instruction, The Associates are therefore of opinion that a Mistress will be preferable to a Master as she may teach the Girls to Sew, knit &c. as well as all to say their Catechism. They think 30 Children or thereabout will sufficiently employ one person, & therefore would at present confine their School to about that number. I need not inform You that it is their Desire the Expence may be as small as the nature of the Design & proper Encouragement of it will admit. Hope 15£ or 16£ a Year may suffice; but desire You will not exceed 20£ Sterling. They are unwilling to suppose that any persons in Your Province will disapprove of this pious Undertaking, but hope that all Objections will be silenced by the School's being put under the Care & Patronage of such

FEBRUARY 29, 1760, PAGE 1: Rev. John Waring, the long-serving secretary of the Bray Associates, created a sense of moral urgency in establishing a school to instruct Black children in the principles of Christianity, "with all convenient speed." *(John Waring to Rev. Dawson, February 29, 1760, Tracy W. McGregor Library of American History, Albert and Shirley Small Special Collections Library, University of Virginia)*

persons & that all prejudices against instructing the Negroes will gradualy die away, as tis hoped the good Effects of this School will every day become more & more apparent.

The Associates presuming on Your kind Assistance have sent a Box of Books for the Use of the School, besides which there is a Folio Volume, a Present from the Associates to Your College Library. There are likewise 5 Copies of Mr Bacons Sermons on this Subject which may be useful to lend to such Masters who do not seem sufficiently apprized how much it is their Duty to take Care that their Slaves especialy those born in their houses be instructed in the principles of Christianity.

I am directed to request the Favour of a Letter from You as soon as the School is opened, & that You will from time to time send Us an Account of the State of the School, the number of each Sex admitted, the Progress they make in their Reading & Catechism &c.

About a Year & Quarter ago a School was opened at Philadelphia for 30 black Children on the Associates Account; which met with a very Favourable Reception. The Desire of the Masters to have their black Children instructed, The Progress the Children have made & their decent behaviour give great Satisfaction: That School is under the Care & Inspection of the Revd Mr Sturgeon; who requires the Mistress to attend the Children to Church on Wed & Frid & after divine Service he charitably catechises & instructs them.

Mr Franklin of Philadelphia One of the Associates & at present in London intends to write to Mr Hunter on this Subject which He probably will receive about the time this comes to Your hand Be pleased to draw on me for the Salary half Yearly or Quarterly

FEBRUARY 29, 1760, PAGE 2: In his correspondence, Rev. Waring repeatedly appealed to the Christian conscience of Anglican leaders to establish and maintain the Williamsburg school. Note his references to Philadelphia and Benjamin Franklin. *(John Waring to Rev. Dawson, February 29, 1760, Tracy W. McGregor Library of American History, Albert and Shirley Small Special Collections Library, University of Virginia)*

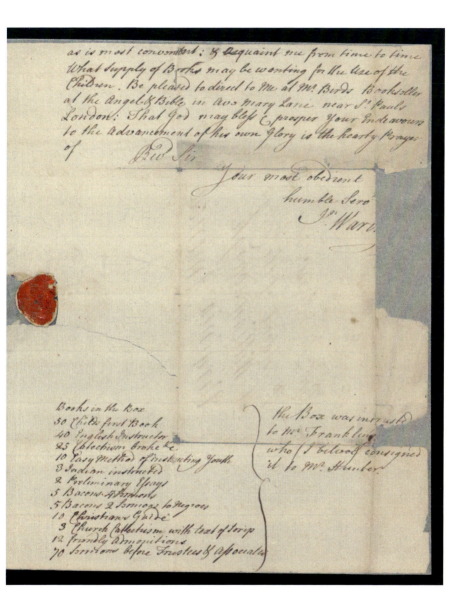

FEBRUARY 29, 1760, PAGE 3: The hundreds of books represented on this list were not the only textbooks sent to the Williamsburg Bray School. Records of the Bray Associates indicate that additional shipments of textbooks were sent in 1761, 1763, and 1771. *(John Waring to Rev. Dawson, February 29, 1760, Tracy W. McGregor Library of American History, Albert and Shirley Small Special Collections Library, University of Virginia)*

Sir,

Wmsburg, Virginia Feb. 16. 1761.

I receiv'd some Time ago a Letter from Mr. Franklin, informing me that I had been nominated as one of the Mannagers of a School to be erected here, for the Education of Negroes in the Christian Faith, &c. — Mr. Dawson, Commissary and Minister of this Parish, received at the same Time your Letter, on the same Subject. We consulted together and agreed with Mrs. Anne Wager for the opening a School at Michaelmas last; which was accordingly done. — We judg'd that the Allowance of £20 Sterling was not sufficient; we gave the Mistress therefore the whole Sum as a Salary, and Mr. Dawson undertook to raise Ten Pounds Sterling by Subscription for the Payment of House Rent: But he dying soon after, nothing has been done to that Purpose; neither do I believe did he ever answer your Letter. — I should have done it sooner myself, but I could not, 'til lately, procure your Letter of his Executor.

As I did not approve of raising the additional Money, by a petty Subscription, I have not attempted it; but am myself liable for the present Year. — I judg'd it more to the Credit of

FEBRUARY 16, 1761, PAGE 1: William Hunter reported the Bray School's 1760 opening on "Michaelmas," a Christian religious holiday that, in Western traditions, is celebrated on September 29. School operations were inextricably tied to the Church of England. *(Bodleian Library, University of Oxford [2024])*

the Associates to pay the whole Expence necessary, than to be aided by a trifling Contribution. — I would therefore recommend it to them to increase the Allowance to £30 Sterling, if they would maintain the School in any tolerable Credit. — And this I think is as little as it can be done for.

I have the Pleasure of informing the Associates that their Design has been generally well received.

The School was opened with 24 Scholars, (as many I think as one Woman can well manage) Their Progress and Improvement in so short a Time, has greatly exceeded my Expectation, and I have Reason to hope that the good Intentions of the Associates will be fully answer'd, by the Care and good Conduct of the Mistress. —

At present I stand single in this Undertaking but Mr Yates being last Week elected Minister of the Parish in the Room of Mr Dawson, I shall communicate to him your Letter, and doubt not his Concurrence. — As it was the Intention of the Associates to nominate three Trustees,

FEBRUARY 16, 1761, PAGE 2: Although later student lists recorded an average of thirty children at school, Ann Wager had an initial class of twenty-four students. Unfortunately, there are no known surviving records to tell us who the first Williamsburg Bray School Scholars were. *(Bodleian Library, University of Oxford [2024])*

not knowing that M.r Dawson was Minister of the Parish, I would recommend a Letter to be written to Rob.t Carter Nicholas Esq.r to whom I have never mention'd it, imagining that a Letter from the Associates would best secure his Compliance.

The Mistress was paid one Quarter's Salary at Christmas, for which I have given M.r Tarpley an Order on you; but may probably for the future draw but once a Year, to prevent the Trouble of small Bills.

Be pleas'd to assure the Associates of my hearty Endeavours to further their good Designs, by making this Establishment, at present in its Infancy, as generally beneficial as possible.

I am, respectfully,
Sir,
Your very h.ble Serv.t
W.m Hunter.

M.r John Waring
at M.r Bird's, Bookseller at the Angel & Bible
in Mary Lane London

FEBRUARY 16, 1761, PAGE 3: Ann Wager was to be paid her teacher's salary in quarterly installments. Subsequent records show that she was compensated in credit, rather than cash, which was a common practice in colonial Virginia. *(Bodleian Library, University of Oxford [2024])*

Sir   Virginia Williamsburg 30th Sepr. 1762

    Agreeable to your request we send you enclosed a List of the Negro Children now at the School under our Direction in this City, with an Account of their Ages as nearly as they can be judged of, but it is not in our Power to determine exactly the Dates of their Admission into the School, inasmuch as some of them having been there ever since it was first opened & others admitted just as Vacancies have happened; the Mistress has not been so exact as to keep any Account of the Times of their Entrances, so that it is impossible for us to give the desired Satisfaction in this Point. You may from hence easily judge how difficult it must be for us to inform you particularly of the Progress each Child has made. We can only say in general that at a late Visitation of the School we were pretty much pleased with the Scholars Performances, they rather exceeded our Expectations. The Children we believe have all been regularly baptized, indeed we think it is a pretty general Practice all over Virginia for the Negro Parents to have their Children Christened, where they live tolerably convenient to the Church or Minister, & sometimes a great Number of Adults are baptized together in different Parts of the Country. We would not have you think, from what was wrote you last Fall, that we had the least Inclination to discourage so good & pious an Institution; we were indeed & still are apprized of many Difficulties which we shall have to struggle with, & were therefore willing in some Measure to prepare you for a disappointment, in case the Undertaking should not answer your Expectations. From the small View we have had of the Associates extensive Charity, we flatter ourselves that we see the Situation of our poor Slaves with respect to their spiritual Concerns, with the same pitious Eyes that they do, & should think ourselves extreamly fortunate, if any Endeavours of ours could contribute towards their Happiness. You no Doubt are already apprized that the Slaves in this & the neighbouring Colonies are the chief Instruments of Labour & we fear that they are treated by too many of their Owners as no more than Beasts of Burthen, as little do they consider them as entitled to any of the Privileges of human Nature, & in as many Owners of Slaves tho' they may view them in a different Light & treat them with a great Degree of Tenderness, concern themselves very little or not at all with their Morals, much less do they trouble themselves with their religious Concerns, so far from it, that we don't think ourselves the least uncharitable in saying that we fear the Negroes are often corrupted & rendered more abandoned by the ill Examples which are set them by many white People in the Country & in inconsiderable Number of these themselves Masters of Slaves. This Observation may be justified by a Comparison of new Negroes when they are first imported with those who have resided amongst us for some Years, for tho' the former no Doubt, bring with them vicious Inclinations & a Number of ill Customs, yet we may venture to say that they contract

SEPTEMBER 30, 1762, PAGE 1: The density of this letter by Robert Carter Nicholas and William Yates to the Bray Associates speaks volumes about how substantial an endeavor the Williamsburg Bray School was. *(Bodleian Library, University of Oxford [2024])*

new Views, which they were Strangers to in their native Country. From this cursory View of the Situation of our Slaves, you may easily judge how extremely difficult it would be if not morally impossible, to work any Thing like a Reformation amongst them, unless some of their Masters & the Generality of white People were first reformed, we had almost said new moulded. We would not have it inferred from hence that we enter into any particular pointed Reflections upon the People of this Country; on the contrary we believe them as good as their Neighbours & think they are much of the same Complexion as the Inhabitants of other Countries. And tho' we almost despair of an entire Reformation, yet we have our Hopes that a Scheme like yours prudently conducted, if it could meet with due Encouragement might have a good Effect. We find that many People in this City upon the first opening of your School were well enough inclined towards it & if their Fund allotted was sufficient we believe that double the Number of Scholars might easily be procured, but at the same Time we fear that many People, who have sent or would send their little Negroes to School, would not do it upon the Principles, which they ought, we mean purely with a View to have them instructed in the Principles of Religion & enabled to instruct their Fellow Slaves at Home. Some People, we fear, send their Children merely to keep them out of Mischief, others to improve them in Hopes, by their being made a little more sensible, that they may be made more handy & useful in their Families; we form this Opinion from observing that several, who put their Negroes to School, have taken them Home again as soon as they began to read, but before they had received any real Benefit or it could be supposed that they were made acquainted with the Principles of Christianity. This is one great Impediment which we are apprehensive will obstruct the Success of our Endeavours. We shall strive to guard against it, tho' we do be with great Difficulty that we shall be able to accomplish our Purpose. Few People have more Negroes than they can employ, & tho' when they are very young & useless, they may be willing to send them to School, yet when they grow up a little & be able to tend their Owners Children or do any other little Offices in their Families they chuse & will take them Home. Another Difficulty, which arises on the Part of the Owners, is that an Opinion prevails amongst many of them, that it might be dangerous & impolitick to enlarge the Understandings of the Negroes, as they would probably by this Means become more impatient of their Slavery & at some future Day be more likely to rebel. They urge further from Experience that it is generally observable that the most sensible of our Slaves are the most wicked & ungovernable; these Observations we think are illy founded, when used as Objections to your Scheme, for he so is by no Means calculated to instruct the Slaves in dangerous Principles, but on the contrary has a probable & direct Tendency to reform their Manners & by making them good Christians they would necessarily become better Servants. We shall not fail in endeavouring to

SEPTEMBER 30, 1762, PAGE 2: Bray School trustees combatted resistance to Black education with the argument that "by making [the enslaved] better Christians they would necessarily become better Servants." (*Bodleian Library, University of Oxford* [2024])

remove Scruples of this Kind or some other Sort, but finding they have taken deep Root in some Minds, we are apprehensive of great Difficulties in overcoming them. There is still one greater Discouragement, which I fear we shall labour under. Tho' the Owners of the Negro Children should chearfully close with our Proposals & submit them entirely to our Government, tho' the Mistress of the School should be ever so diligent in her Duty, & tho' the Scholars should make as great Progress as could be wished, yet we fear that notwithstanding all our Endeavours to prevent it, any good Impressions, which may be made on the Childrens Minds at School, will be too easily effaced by their mixing with other Slaves who are mostly abandoned to every Thing of Wickedness. If evil Communications have a general Tendency to corrupt good Manners, the Observation is nevermore likely to be verified than in Instances of this Sort, where the very Parents of the Children will probably much oftener than others set them bad Examples. Notwithstanding these & many other Difficulties, which the narrow Limits of a Letter will not allow us to particularize, & store us fully in the Face, we are resolved not to be discouraged; but hope by the Blessing of God upon your Charity & our Endeavours that the Undertaking will greatly prosper. The late Reverend Mr Dawson & Mr Hunter, we believe, had it in their Intention to form Rules for the better Government of the School, but were prevented by Death. We have hitherto contented ourselves with permitting the Mistress to exercise her Judgment. The May it was begun, but being sensible that nothing of the Sort can be properly conducted without certain uniform Regulations, by which all Parties concerned may know how to govern themselves, we have drawn up such a Set of Rules as appear to us proper, as ables & send you a Copy of them enclosed for your & the rest of the Associates Approbation & should be glad to know your Sentiments. We shall be willing to add or admonish any Thing as you may advise. We probably shall have Occasion of a few Testaments & spelling Books & perhaps a Number of Mr Bacon's Sermons, recommending the Instruction of Negroes in the Christian Faith, properly dispersed over the County might have a good Influence. I would not put you to the Expence of any other Books at present. We will not conclude without offering our best Respects to you & the rest of the worthy Associates. Believe us, Sir, we can not enough admire a Set of Gentlemen, who at the same Time that they are employed in exercising every Act of Benevolence at Home, have so far enlarged their Charity as to extend it to the most distant Colonies. We are, Sir, with the greatest Esteem

Copy of a Letter sent by another
opportunity.

Y.r most ob.t h.ble Serv.ts
Ro. C. Nicholas & Self
and Mr Wm Yates.

A List of Negro Children at the School established by the Associates of the late Revrnd Doctr Bray in the City of Williamsburg — Mrs Anne Wager — School Mistress.

Names of the Children	their Ages as near as can be judged of	Owners Names
1 John	8 Years	Mr Davenport
2 Anne	6	Do
3 Dick	3	Mr George Davenport
4 London	7	Mr Campbell
5 Aggy	6	Do
6 Shropshire	6	Do
7 Aberdeen	5	Mr Alexr Craig
8 Mary	7	Mr Thomas Everard
9 Harry	5	Do
10 George	8	Mr Gilmer
11 Bristol	7	Do
12 Mary Anne	7	a free Negro
13 Aggy	7	Peyton Randolph Esqr
14 Roger	7	Do
15 Mary	8	Mr Thomas Hornsby
16 Pippin	3	Mr Anthony Hay
17 Robert	6	John Randolph Esqr
18 Lucy	5	Do
19 Elizabeth	10	Mrs Dawson
20 George	6	Dr James Carter
21 Lewis	8	Mr Armistead
22 Sarah	7	Mrs Page
23 Hannah	7	Ro. C. Nicholas
24 Mary Jones		a free Negro
25 John	7	John Blair Esqr
26 Jane	9	Do
27 Doll	7	Do
28 Elisha Jones		free
29 John	3	Mr Hugh Orr
30 Phœbe	3	Mr Wm Trebell

Wmsburg 30th Septr 1762

copy

SEPTEMBER 30, 1762, PAGE 4: The earliest attendance report of Williamsburg Bray School students, this 1762 list is the only one known to include the students' ages. It is also the first report to list free Black children in attendance: Mary and Elisha Jones, and Mary Anne. *(Bodleian Library, University of Oxford [2024])*

The Associates of the late Reverend Doctor Bray, residing in England, having established Schools in several of the Northern Colonies for the Education of Negroes in the Principles of the Christian Religion & teaching them to read, & at the same time rendering the Females more useful to their Owners by instructing them in sewing, knitting &c. encouraged by the Success of these their pious Endeavours & being solicitous to make this Kind of Charity as extensive as possible, they some time ago came to a Resolution of establishing a School in the City of Williamsburg for the same purpose & have thought fit to recommend it to the immediate Care & Government of the Revd Mr William Yates & Mr Robert Carter Nicholas who have chearfully undertaken the Trust & it is hoped that all good Christians will co-operate with them in their Endeavours to promote the success of so laudable & pious an Institution.

The Associates having engaged in so many Works of this Kind, which will require a very considerable Sum of Money to defray the Expence of, have limited the Number of Scholars to thirty, but as there may be many more Negro Children in this City equally Objects of such a Charity the Trustees will thankfully accept of any Contributions which may be offered, towards augmenting the Number & thereby rendering the Scheme more generally beneficial. If the Scholars should encrease so as to make it necessary they propose to employ another Mistress, And for the Satisfaction of their Benefactors they will be at all times ready to give an account of their Proceedings.

The Trustees for the better Government of the School & to render it truly beneficial have thought fit to establish certain Regulations, relating as well to the Owners of Slaves as to the Teacher or Mistress, which they are resolved to have strictly observed & put in Execution, unless they should at any time hereafter be induced by good Reasons to alter or relax them.

With respect to the Owners

The School being at present full with the Number of Scholars proposed to be educated at the Expence of the Associates, such Masters or Mistresses who may incline hereafter to send their Negro Children to the School are desired to signify the same to the Trustees as they would choose hereafter that all vacancies should be filled up by an equal Number from each Family as near as may be.

SEPTEMBER 30, 1762, PAGE 5: To promote consistency at the Bray School, trustees outlined the obligations of its various stakeholders, including those who legally owned the enslaved children sent there. (*Bodleian Library, University of Oxford [2024]*)

SEPTEMBER 30, 1762, PAGE 6: Bray School instruction was to include Anglican teachings, spelling, reading, and having the children "mind their stops"—marks or punctuation that distinguished sentences. *(Bodleian Library, University of Oxford [2024])*

3. She shall make it her principal Care to teach them to read the Bible, to instruct them in the Principles of the Christian Religion according to the Doctrines of the Church of England, & shall explain the Church Catechism to them by some good Expositions, which, together with the Catechism, they shall publickly repeat in Church or elsewhere, so often as the Trustees shall require & shall be frequently examined in School, as to their Improvements of every Sort.

4. She shall teach them those Doctrines & Principles of Religion which are in their Nature most useful in the Course of private Life, especially such as concern Faith & good Manners.

5. She shall conduct them from her School House, where they are all to be first assembled, in a decent & orderly Manner to Church so often as divine Service is there performed, & before it begins instruct & oblige them to behave in a proper Manner, kneeling or standing as the Rubrick directs, & to join in the public Service with it & regularly to repeat after the Minister in all Places where the People are so directed & in such a Manner as not to disturb the rest of the Congregation. She shall take Care that the Scholars, as soon as they are able to use them, do carry their Bibles & Prayer Books to Church with them, & that they may be prevented from spending the Lord's Day profanely or idly. She shall give her Scholars some Task out of the most useful Parts of Scripture, to be learnt on each Lord's Day, according to their Capacities & shall require a strict Performance of it every Monday Morning.

6. She shall use proper Prayers in her School every Morning & Evening & teach the Scholars to do the same at Home, devoutly on their Knees, and also teach them to say Grace before & after eating their Victuals, explaining to them the Design & Meaning of it.

7. She shall take particular Care of the Manners & Behaviour of her Scholars & by all proper Methods discourage Idleness & suppress the Beginnings of Vice, such as lying, cursing, swearing, profaning the Lord's Day, obscene Discourse, stealing &c. putting them often in Mind & obliging them to get by Heart such Parts of the Holy Scriptures where these Things are forbid & where Christians are commanded to be faithful & obedient to their Masters, to be diligent in their Business, & quiet & peaceable to all Men.

8. She shall teach her Female Scholars knitting, sewing & such other Things as may be useful to their Owners & she shall be particularly watchful that her Scholars between the School Hours do not commit any Irregularities nor fall into any indecent

SEPTEMBER 30, 1762, PAGE 7: Ann Wager's teaching responsibilities were exhaustive. Her days started early, and although students did not live at the school, she had daily charge of thirty children. *(Bodleian Library, University of Oxford [2024])*

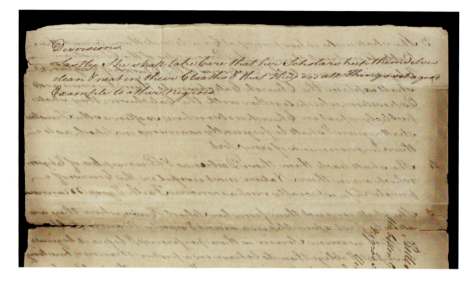

SEPTEMBER 30, 1762, PAGE 8: Bray School students' outward appearances were important to trustees, as was their perceived inner conversion. Ann Wager was charged with keeping the young scholars "clean & neat in their Cloathes," so they might be good examples to their peers. *(Bodleian Library, University of Oxford [2024])*

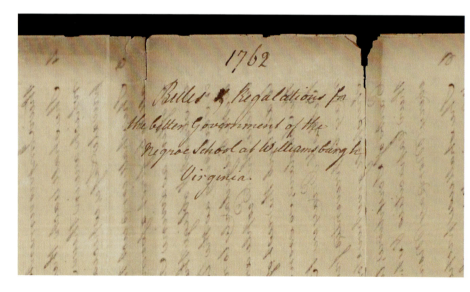

SEPTEMBER 30, 1762, ENVELOPE: The Williamsburg Bray School was alternately referred to as the "Negro School" or the "Charity School." *(Bodleian Library, University of Oxford [2024])*

Williamsburg in Virg.ᵃ 27.ᵗʰ Dec.ʳ 1765.

Rev.ᵈ Sir:

I send you inclosed a List of the Negro Children who belong to the Charity School in this City. It is impossible for me to fix their Ages, but I suppose them to be from about four to ten Years; the Times of their Standing at School, from the Mistress's Acc.ᵗ which she has not kept with any Scrupulous Exactness, are from about six Months to two or two & an half Years. The Rules which I formerly drew up for the better Government of this School & which you & the other Associates were pleased to approve, I would gladly have executed, but soon found that the Masters & Mistresses were so averse to every thing that looks like Compulsion, that I thought it most adviseable to relax a little, in hopes that Things might be put upon a more agreeable Footing. You'll observe there are thirty four Children in the List, which exceeds the Number, which the Mistress engaged to teach; it is not in her Power to oblige them to give a constant Attendance & therefore, I believe, she is willing to instruct all such as offer themselves; The Owners of Negroes as soon as they are old enough to do little Offices about their Houses, either take them away entirely from the School, or keep them from it at Times, so that they only attend, when there is no Employment for them at Home. The Term which

DECEMBER 27, 1765, PAGE 1: Robert Carter Nicholas reported that students attended "from about six Months to two or two & an half years." This disparity in student attendance patterns fueled tensions between Nicholas, other enslavers, and the Bray Associates. *(Bodleian Library, University of Oxford [2024])*

I proposed for the Children to continue at School was three Years at least; few are allow'd to stay so long, but those, who do, generally learn to read pretty well & learn their Prayers & Catechism, tho' I fear that most of the good Principles, which they are taught at School, are soon effaced, when they get Home by the bad Examples set them there & for want of the Instructions necessary to confirm them in those Principles. I have a Negro Girl in my Family, who was taught at this School upwards of three Years & made as good a Progress as most, but she turns out a sad Jade, notwithstanding all we can do to reform her. I am heartily glad to hear of the Success of your charitable Endeavours in the Northern Provinces; they have but few Negroes in those Places compared with the Number in Virginia & therefore I suppose they are not so much abandon'd. I have lately visited the School here & examin'd the Children, who seem to have made a reasonable Progress; the Mistress is pretty far advanced in Years & I am afraid that the Business will soon be too laborious for her, & how to supply the School better I don't know. I am satisfied that she takes a great deal of Pains with the Children & I shall not fail to encourage her & do every thing in my Power to promote the Success of so pious an Institution.

DECEMBER 27, 1765, PAGE 2: It is likely that Hannah was the "Negro Girl in my Family" whom Robert Carter Nicholas enslaved and described. She appeared on the 1762 student list and would have been about ten years old when Nicholas wrote this letter. *(Bodleian Library, University of Oxford [2024])*

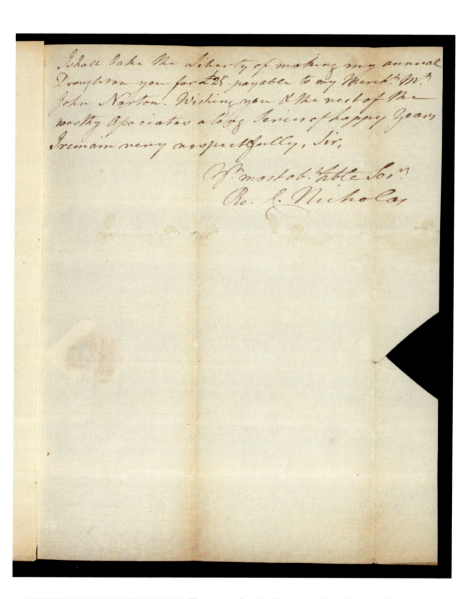

DECEMBER 27, 1765, PAGE 3: Treasurer for the Virginia colony, Robert Carter Nicholas kept careful records of when and how funds were expended to support the purportedly pious designs of the Williamsburg Bray School. *(Bodleian Library, University of Oxford [2024])*

A List of Negro Children who are at the Charity School in Williamsburg Nov.r 1765

Mrs. Campbell's young & Mary	2
Mr. Davenport's William	1
Mr. Hay's Jerry	1
Doctr. Carter's Nanny	1
Mr. Blair's John, Dolly, Elizabeth, Catherine, Fanny, Isaac & Johanna	7
Mr. Burwell's Joseph & Davy	2
Mr. Prentis's Molly	1
Colo. Johnson's Squire	1
Colo. Chiswell's Edmund & Johnny	2
Mr. Charlton's Nancy & Davy	2
Mr. Grymes's Phillis	1
Mr. Orr's Patt & Jack, James & Sal	4
Mr. Thompson's Charles	1
Mr. Brown's Elizabeth	1
Mr. Thompson's Betty	1
Matt. Ashby's Harry & John	2
Mr. Vobe's Sal	1
Mr. Waters's Sylvia	1
Mr. Randolph's Roger & Sam	2
in all	34

DECEMBER 27, 1765, PAGE 4: The Ashbys, another free Black family, also sent their children—John, Mary, and Harry—to the Bray School. This raises questions about how free children navigated the school's pro-slavery ethos. *(Bodleian Library, University of Oxford [2024])*

Rev.d Sir. Williamsburg in Virg.a 16.th February 1769.

I have received both your late Letters & am sorry to find you expressing the least Dissatisfaction at my Conduct with Respect to the Negro School in this City, the Success of which I have done every Thing in my Power to promote. When I first engaged in this Business, tho' I could not but very cordially commend the pious Designs of its Authors, yet I was aware of the many Difficulties it might meet with & therefore communicated them to you freely & without Reserve. I formerly sent you a List of the Negro Children at School & could only in general observe that I thought they were properly attended to & had made as good a Progress as I expected, all Things consider'd. I don't know what farther Information I can give; the Children are so often shifted that it would be almost endless to attempt giving you the Dates of their Entries & Times of leaving the School. The Regulations which I formerly drew up & transmitted to you, I was in hopes of carrying into Execution, but have been disappointed in several Respects. I send you a List of the Children now at School & another of those who have left it. The Books you sent I have taken Care of; the Mistress has such as she wants from Time, & I have occasionally lent & given others of them to grown Negroes in different Parts, who I thought would make a good Use of them; this measure I consider'd as cooperating with your principal Design, & hope you will approve of it. It gives me Pain that you should suppose I had exceeded your Limits so far as you mention. You may remember that I succeeded M.r Hunter in this Business & of course must have conform'd to your Directions to him, when not alter'd by subsequent Instructions to me. Give me leave to quote a Passage or two from M.r Letter to him of the 1.st of June 1761. viz.t "They (meaning the Associates) acknowledge that they "are not competent Judges what Salary may be sufficient "for a Mistress & therefore must refer that Matter intirely "to your Prudence & Discretion, but as they paid no more "than £20 St.g for 30 Children both at Philadelphia & "New York City, they hoped the same Stipend might be "sufficient with you, however that this Undertaking may "meet with no Check or Discouragement in its Infancy

---

FEBRUARY 16, 1769, PAGE 1: Tensions ran high between Williamsburg and London as Robert Carter Nicholas defended his leadership amid the Bray Associates' dissatisfaction with finances and attendance. *(Bodleian Library, University of Oxford [2024])*

"on this Account, they have directed me to acquaint you
"that they chearfully increase their Appointment
"to £30 Stg, not doubting, but in Time a Proposal for a
"Subscription towards its Support will be favourably
"received at Williamsburg. In the mean while they would
"be glad the Number of Scholars were increased to
"30 agreeable to their first Proposal & to the Number
"instructed in their other Schools &c." The Number of
Scholars was at first, as I understood, only 24; this Letter
coming to my Hands, soon after Mr. Hunter's Death,
I had the Number increased to 30 & obliged the Mistress,
that there might be no partiality shewn to white Scholars,
of which she then had about a dozen, to discharge them
all & this at the Risque of the Displeasure of their
Parents, with whom she was in high Repute for
her Care & Method of teaching. Having this Letter for
my guide & Direction, you may easily judge at my Sur:
:prize to find you complaining that I had advanced
the Salary to £25 Stg without proper Authority. Mr. Prentis
had fix'd the Mistress's Salary at £5 a Quarter, a Sum,
for 30 Scholars, much less than is paid for Schooling in
this City to other Mistresses; but, as Mrs. Wager
had no House of her own, she was at first allow'd
£8 Curr.y Money more to pay for the Rent of a House,
which was much too small for such a Number of
Children; however she continued in it as long as it
was tenantable; I was then obliged to rent the House,
where she now resides, of Mr. President Blair, for
twelve Pounds Curr.y Money. My first Bills were only
for £25 Stg; this did pretty well with my advancing,
generally, a Yr's Salary before I drew the Bills & when
our Exch.e was at 55. 60. 60 & 40 PC.t; but, when Exch.e
fell to 25 PC.t, you see that £30 Stg yielded not enough
to pay the Salary & Rent; if you'll be pleased to calculate,
you will find that my Draughts upon an Average are con:
:siderably under £30 Stg besides that I have generally been
considerably in advance, a Circumstance, which I
never regarded & should not mention it, but upon this
Occasion. As to raising Money by Subscription, I have
sounded many of the Inhabitants, but never had the
least Encouragement to hope for Success in such a Scheme.
I have still ventured to continue the School upon the old Foot:
:ing, till I know the Associates' further Pleasure, after they

have been made thoroughly acquainted with the whole Matter & reconsider'd it. I have my hopes that they will think there is some Consideration due to the Mistress, who has actually thrown herself out of other Business by engaging in this. I could not at any Rate discontinue any Part of the Allowance before the first of Jan'y last, as both she & her House were engaged for the Year certain. I think, that I before sent you my Acc.t to Dec.r 1766, when I drew for £37.10. the exact Bal: then due to me; I send you now my further Acc.t by which it will appear that there is now due to me £42.10 curr'y Money, for which I have drawn on you to my Friend Mr. Norton, & can have no Doubt of it's meeting with due Hon.r If there should be any Mistake in the Acc.t, it shall be immediately rectified upon being pointed out. You have forgot another thing I mean the Death of my very worthy Friend the Rev.d Mr. Yates, who left us several Years ago, of which I soon after advised you. I am very resp[ectfully]
Sir,
Y.r mo. ob.t Serv.t
R. C. Nicholas

FEBRUARY 16, 1769, PAGE 3: Despite a strained relationship with the school's benefactors, Robert Carter Nicholas remained the Bray Associates' "most obedient servant," resigned to the administrative task at hand. *(Bodleian Library, University of Oxford [2024])*

Negroes now at School.

Mrs. Prisca. Dawson's Grace	1
Mr. R. C. Nicholas's Sarah	1
Mr. Presid.t Blair's Cathne, Nancy, Jan & Clara Bee	4
Mr. Hay's Jenny, Joseph, Dick	3
Mr. Chiswell's Jack	1
Mr. Campbell's Mary, Sally, Sukey	3
Mr. Speaker's Sam	1
Mr. Nobe's Jack	1
John & Mary Ashby — free	2
Mr. Ayscough's Sally	1
The College. Adam, Fany	2
The Commissary's Charlotte	1
Mrs. Blaikley's Jenny, Jack	2
Hon. Rob.t Carter's Dennis	1
Mr. Hornsby's Nancy, Judy, Ratchel	3
Mr. Cocke's Mourning	1
Mr. Davenport's Matt, Fany	2

FEBRUARY 16, 1769, PAGE 4: Although the Williamsburg Bray School operated for another five years, this is the last known extant report of students in attendance. *(Bodleian Library, University of Oxford [2024])*

Virginia 17th Nov.r 1774

Rev.d Sir,

I have to advise you of the Death of Mrs. Wager, the Mistress of the Negro School at Williamsburg. I could wish to have revived the Charity upon such Terms as would be agreeable to you & the rest of the worthy Associates of D.r Bray, but seeing no Prospect of it at present, I have discontinued the School, 'till I can receive your farther Directions. The Acc.t of what I am in Advance you will receive inclos:ed, Bal.a in my favo.r £11.17.2, for which I have drawn on you in favo.r of Mess.rs Norton & Sons.

Wishing you & the rest of the Associates every Felicity, I remain very respectfully,
Rev.d Sir,
Y.r mo. ob.t Serv.t
Ro. C. Nicholas

Agreed that Thanks be returned to Rob.t C. N. for that they acquiesce in his Opinion to discontinue the school, & that he be informed the Associates will at any time be very thankful to him for his Directions how their pious Intentions may be most effectually promoted

11

NOVEMBER 17, 1774, PAGE 1: Robert Carter Nicholas advised the Bray Associates of the death of Ann Wager and the subsequent closing of the Williamsburg Bray School. Based on Nicholas's record of salary payments and the absence of other known documents, scholars point to August 20, 1774, as Wager's date of death. (*Bodleian Library, University of Oxford [2024]*)

NOVEMBER 17, 1774, ACCOUNT: Robert Carter Nicholas submitted this final accounting of Williamsburg Bray School financial activity to the Associates of Dr. Bray in late 1774. *(Bodleian Library, University of Oxford [2024])*

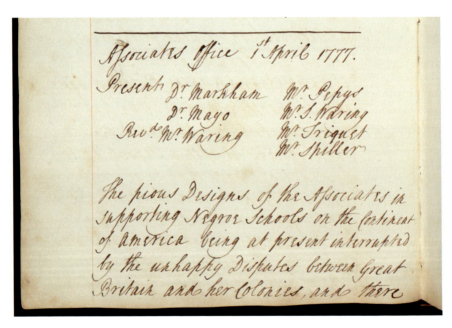

APRIL 1, 1777, BRAY ASSOCIATES MEETING NOTES, PAGE 1: The worlds of former Williamsburg Bray School students were being remade amid the fracturing of empire that was the American Revolution. *(Bodleian Library, University of Oxford [2024])*

being little Prospect of resuming the same, till an amicable Accommodation shall take place

Agreed, that in order to answer the pious Intention of our Association it will be adviseable to adopt some other Plan of Charity of a similar Nature, and this Board are of Opinion the Establishment and Support of Schools in England for the Instruction of poor Children in such Places as shall appear to stand most in need of such charitable Institutions will best correspond with the Intentions of this Society.

The Secretary laid before the Board several Letters from the Revd. Mr. Evans, Curate of Kingswood in Glostershire, setting forth that there are in his Parish about 340 poor Children brought up in profound Ignorance and Immorality, and that he had been encouraged by the assurance of some Subscriptions to open a School for their Instruction, and that 60 or 70 constantly attended, and he had the Prospect of doing much good in the Parish

Agreed to take Mr. Evans's School under the Patronage and Protection of this Society, and that he be assured, that if

APRIL 1, 1777, BRAY ASSOCIATES MEETING NOTES, PAGE 2: In light of dramatic developments in the Atlantic World, the Bray Associates reoriented their religious philanthropy and focused on serving poor children in Great Britain. *(Bodleian Library, University of Oxford [2024])*

BRAY-DIGGES HOUSE: The building that housed the Williamsburg Bray School is shown in its original Prince George Street location in a photograph likely taken in the early 1920s. *(Special Collections, John D. Rockefeller Jr. Library, The Colonial Williamsburg Foundation)*

MOVING DAY: The original 18th-century home of the Williamsburg Bray School makes the slow journey from the William & Mary campus, past its historical marker, to the corner of Nassau and Francis streets on February 10, 2023. *(Grace Helmick, Strategic Cultural Partnerships, William & Mary)*

REMEMBERING THE STUDENTS: Local schoolchildren hold signs bearing the names of known Williamsburg Bray School Scholars as the house makes its way to its new location in Colonial Williamsburg's Historic Area. *(The Colonial Williamsburg Foundation)*

VISITING THE SCHOOL: Descendants of the Williamsburg Bray School Scholars tour the building's new site after the structure was carefully placed on a new brick foundation. *(Grace Helmick, Strategic Cultural Partnerships, William & Mary)*

PEELING THE LAYERS: The original 1760 firebox located on the second floor was uncovered after years of being sealed. Rats' nests found inside yielded 19th- and 20th-century artifacts. *(The Colonial Williamsburg Foundation)*

ORIGINAL PIECES: The 1760 staircase (left) would have been used by the Williamsburg Bray School teacher, Ann Wager, to get to the second floor. Its original banister (right) remains intact. *(The Colonial Williamsburg Foundation)*

RECONSTRUCTION: Kevin Nieto, a contract master mason, rebuilds the chimney stack on the west end of the building. The original chimney was lost in 1930. *(The Colonial Williamsburg Foundation)*

UNUSUAL FIND: Pieces of iron were sometimes included in the molding of bricks, likely to help harden them during the firing process. It is rare to find formed iron, like these nails found in the wall of the building. *(The Colonial Williamsburg Foundation)*

A QUICK FIX: An 18th-century carpenter fixed a loose, and likely squeaking stair, by pushing nails into the gap of the tread. *(The Colonial Williamsburg Foundation)*

UNCOVERING ORIGINALS: Colonial Williamsburg Architectural Preservation Technician Scott Merrifield removes comparatively modern floorboards to expose the original flooring. *(The Colonial Williamsburg Foundation)*

MAKING PROGRESS: Construction proceeded in early 2024 on the second floor of the building and its roof. *(The Colonial Williamsburg Foundation)*

FURNISHING THE SCHOOL: By the spring of 2024, work was underway on the interior elements for the school, including a chair made by Colonial Williamsburg's Historic Trades Master Joiner Brian Weldy. *(The Colonial Williamsburg Foundation)*

STUDENTS' BOOKS: Colonial Williamsburg Journeyman Supervisor Peter Stinley prepares blocks of text for printing replicas of "The Child's First Book," which is known to have been used in the Williamsburg Bray School classroom. *(The Colonial Williamsburg Foundation)*

Asking Hard Questions

An essay by Yvonne L. "Bonnie" Johnson

Just like the Williamsburg Bray School was hidden in plain sight, the Bray Scholars' stories are coming to life—not through their voices, but, in part, through the Bray School Descendant Community sharing its thoughts and feelings about the letters written by the school's administrators.

Many enslavers thought it was a waste of time and money to educate African Americans because they thought they were only fit to labor in the fields or serve their families domestically. There was also the real fear that educating enslaved children kindled a fire of freedom and resistance that was inherently dangerous in a slave society. However, there were some who accepted that it was their Christian duty to teach enslaved children to be good, obedient servants and to instruct them in the catechism of the Church of England.

Robert Carter Nicholas, in the most respectful manner he was able, managed to convey how offended he was about being questioned over his financial stewardship of Bray Associates funding. In his letter of February 16, 1769, Nicholas referenced an earlier 1761 letter from the Bray Associates to William Hunter, acknowledging that they were not competent judges of what salary would be sufficient for securing a teacher like Ann Wager to teach an initial class of twenty-four girls and boys. As history tells us, that number soon rose to thirty students, but the Bray Associates felt that if £20 could secure a teacher of thirty children in Philadelphia and New York City, it would suffice for Williamsburg.

Robert Carter Nicholas took it upon himself to increase Ann Wager's salary to £25 without the Associates' authorization. Wager was a widow and the rent on the modest house in which she lived and taught thirty children was paid by local trustees, like Nicholas, using Bray Associates funding. Bray School trustees hoped that the benefactors would take into consideration the fact that Ann Wager's commitment to this assignment took her out of the running for any other job. With the sudden death of William Hunter, Wager's livelihood was put in increased jeopardy. This sounds familiar, with many of today's teachers spending their own money to purchase classroom supplies and reducing their already modest salaries.

In this 1769 correspondence, Robert Carter Nicholas could not account for the comings and goings of the Bray Scholars because the children were shifted based on the changing needs of their enslavers. He attached with his 1769 letter the list of thirty students then at school. Although he promised a list of those who had left, such an accounting has yet to be found and may not have survived. If still extant, this additional student list would be invaluable in expanding our understanding of patterns of Bray School enrollment, attendance, and attrition.

My first job was with Colonial Williamsburg where I sold tickets in the very buildings where the Bray Scholars lived, worked, or passed on their way to school. I think about this as I reflect on the students. How did the Bray School Scholars feel about having the opportunity to attend school? Did they feel proud to be singled out to learn to read and spell while other members of their families did not? Who was the teacher's pet? I can envision Ann Wager teaching the children to read, instructing them daily in Christian principles, and lining them up in single file and parading them to Bruton Parish with their Bibles and prayer books on Sundays. In church, they recited their catechisms before their enslavers as if they were performers on a stage. How did the Bray Scholars feel about their performance?

We have so many questions about the school and its operations, and so few answers. Did Ann Wager have to break up fights? How were the children disciplined? Were they whipped? Did they stand in the corner or face some other type of humiliation? How were they able to share what they read with their families? What was their understanding of servitude in the Bible? How aware were they of the political atmosphere as Virginia moved closer to revolution?

As we approach the 250th anniversary of our nation, it seems we have not learned from past mistakes. There is a move today not to address the painful parts of history. Variations of what is going on today—including destroying books and humanizing artificial intelligence (AI)—played out in movies I remember as a child. What happened in the past cannot be undone. We all need to put on our thick skin and come to terms with it because grappling with the past can be difficult, but not impossible. The only way to heal is to reveal the truth and do better.

Yvonne L. "Bonnie" Johnson is a Bray School Descendant Community member and historian of the Hundley family. "To my ancestors, your story matters. It is my honor to speak and make your voice heard."

Progress: What Did It Mean for the Williamsburg Bray School Scholar?

An essay by Janise Parker

Robert Carter Nicholas began his February 1769 letter with an acknowledgment of the Bray Associates' discontent over the operation of the Williamsburg Bray School, or, in his own words, their "Dissatisfaction at any Conduct with Respect to the Negro School in this City." Nicholas later noted that although he was "aware of the many difficulties it might meet with," his observations of the Bray School children led him to believe that they were making "as good a Progress" as expected. Nevertheless, Nicholas did not detail how he came to the conclusion that the children were making progress or the specific difficulties the Black scholars may have endured.

Overall, I approach the idea of progress in this letter with both skepticism and curiosity. Skepticism leads me to question whether the full story was being told regarding the Williamsburg Bray School students' progress, including the roots of their challenges. Curiosity compels me to dig deeper and ask more questions to understand whose progress Nicholas was *really* referring to—the students' personal growth or the goals of an oppressive system (e.g., the students' compliance to enslavement)—and whether he ever acknowledged chattel slavery as having a robust influence on the students' outcomes.

My first reflection leads me to ponder how the Bray School trustees determined whether the Black children were making progress. Like education today, where *academic achievement* is typically the priority, this letter signifies that the children may have initially acquired or improved their English literacy skills but did not demonstrate consistent growth in the specific areas that Ann Wager desired. Returning to the potential impact of chattel slavery, one wonders whether the children were given adequate time to practice their skills in their home environments to retain all that they had learned, or whether the competing demands of forced labor precluded extended practice from occurring.

At the same time, school mental health professionals in the twenty-first century have advocated for a more holistic approach to understanding student progress by also attending to their *emotional* and *mental well-being*. Students who are emotionally and mentally well are likely to experience academic success. Thus, I wonder whether Williamsburg Bray School trustees accounted for the Black students' mental well-being when assessing the outcomes of the school. Did they observe clusters of Black children that appeared somber and nonchalant from time to time? Alternately, did they make note of the extent to which the children smiled, laughed, and demonstrated other indicators of joy? And how was this maintained? Or did it even matter? If the students' progress was determined by their emotional state and overall well-being, perhaps Robert Carter Nicholas observed initial indicators of happiness and positivity among the children, but a gradual shift in their demeanor contributed to the Bray Associates' "dissatisfaction."

Student voice is critical for understanding how their "inner worlds" of mental well-being interacted with the "outer world." Hence, this notion of progress would have taken on new meaning if the Bray School Scholars were permitted to vocalize what they were experiencing. If limited academic achievement was a concern, perhaps the children would have explained how their thoughts and feelings contributed to such observations. For example, I would imagine that if given the opportunity, the older children would have shared how their growing awareness of the world around them—afforded by their access to a formal education—made them feel even more remorseful about their conditions as oppressed people. They would have expressed the difficulties—anger, frustration, limited motivation—they encountered when trying to digest Eurocentric instruction that eradicated their history as people of the African diaspora.

Perhaps the children lamented over their emerging consciousness of how white supremacy manipulated Christianity to justify chattel slavery. The children may have demonstrated that their education had sparked a more liberated way of thinking that inspired them to find ways to undermine the institution of slavery. This would have contested the adherence to social oppression that white supremacy expected them to show. Collectively, these scenarios would have expanded the depth to which the trustees understood the dynamics surrounding the progress, or lack thereof, among the Williamsburg Bray School students.

Moreover, if the link between social oppression, holistic well-being, and educational success was appreciated by the Bray School trustees, as scholars understand it today, would the trustees have been willing to advocate for the end of slavery? As we continue to learn from the past to create a present that is more socially just, this could have set a much-needed precedent for how K-12 schools should operate today when responding to Black children's educational progress: being willing to dismantle oppressive systems so that all students can thrive.

Janise Parker, PhD, is an associate professor in the School Psychology program in the William & Mary School of Education. As a licensed psychologist and nationally certified school psychologist, Parker takes a healing approach in all she does to inform services that help communities thrive and grow. Much of Parker's work focuses on the intersection of spirituality, religiosity, community support, and mental health in the lives of marginalized youth. She has served as an Office of Strategic Cultural Partnerships Faculty Fellow, working with the William & Mary Bray School Lab.

The Legacy That Haunts:
Our Continued Struggle for Racial Justice in Education

An essay by Jacqueline Bridgeforth-Williams

These Williamsburg Bray School letters haunt me. The voices that spoke for our children and decided their needs were not the voices of their parents or their community. They were the voices of others. The legacy of slavery continues to haunt us, and it continues to haunt our educational system.

I can imagine the Bray School students' great joy at the thought of school. Just the idea of a school to educate Black children during slavery offered such hope. I saw glimpses of that hope in the letter: reports of books being distributed, and student progress evaluated as favorable. But this hope soon dimmed as I read further. I began to imagine the students' great disappointment when the experience of that school was not what they envisioned—in ways we will never fully know.

Indeed, as I read the February 1769 letter by Robert Carter Nicholas, my heart was pulled between the hope that these children encountered the joy of learning and the despair that the broader institutions of white supremacy limited their ability to realize such pleasure. The letter began with these warning signs. Nicholas deflected the Bray Associates' apparent "Dissatisfaction...with Respect to the Negro School" by insisting they had been made aware of "the many Difficulties it might meet with" from the very beginning. Some of these difficulties and reasons for despair are hinted to us in the letter by the report that "the

Children are so often shifted" that "it would be almost endless to attempt giving you the Dates of their Entries and Times of leaving the School."

These legacies haunt us. Almost two centuries after this letter was written, my mother was given old, tattered, used textbooks in the segregated school system in Williamsburg. The institutions of white supremacy remained in place, if in a somewhat different form. Nonetheless, my mother was an astounding student. As her classmates and teachers recall, my mother knew those tattered textbooks from front to back. Her teachers at Bruton Heights supported her and wanted to see her succeed as they did with each of their students. And that made the difference.

These inequities haunt us right now. Over two-and-a-half centuries after this letter was written, our children still do not have equal access to the programs, resources, and books that they need—books that celebrate our community and culture; books with characters that look like our children and tell our stories. What would that look like for students at the Bray School? Was there anyone willing to keep pushing harder for the children and continue their education at all costs? I imagine the feelings of the enslaved children and what the shifting of the students mentioned in the letter meant.

As a member of the Bray School Descendant Community, I further understand the connection between the inequities in education then and today, and the importance of the things we do to address this haunting history. I am the founder and director of The Village Initiative, a grassroots, nonprofit organization devoted to achieving racial justice and equity in the local school system today. I started The Village in 2016, after I learned of the senseless murder of a young African American man whose family I had known for many years. In response to a prayer for guidance, God sent me a vision of a community organization dedicated to educational equity for all children.

A small group of supporters soon responded to my call to action on social media to address the persistent "opportunity gap" that Black children face in schools, and to eliminate the school-to-prison pipeline that results from the disproportionate disciplining of Black and brown children. Over time, The

Village's message spread and inspired community members to come together weekly, to meet in churches, restaurants, and coffee shops, and talk about how to make this vision a reality.

I draft this essay as the Supreme Court ends affirmative action in higher education admission decisions and destroys a powerful effort to address the legacies of slavery today. Like those students at the Bray School, we still have fewer resources and fewer opportunities for a fair educational system. We continue to be pained. You cannot deny that discrimination, separation, and inequity have long plagued our educational system. We are still fighting today. How do we finally move beyond these haunting legacies? We can draw from the hope of the children of the Bray School, and the hope of the children today to ensure that this legacy comes out of the dark and into the light for all children. We, as The Village Initiative, carry the spirit of hope with us as we expand our work and remain true to our core vision of equity and justice. In the words of former President Barack Obama, "We are the change that we seek."

Jacqueline Bridgeforth-Williams is the founder and executive director of The Village Initiative, a nonprofit organization focused on educational equity in the Williamsburg-James City County (WJCC) school system. "I would like to dedicate this essay to my father, the late Russell Bridgeforth, Sr., and my mother, Ellen Bridgeforth—my dear beloveds who inspire me every day to work for the greater good of humanity by striving to be a good ancestor."

Virginia 17th Nov.r 1774

Rev.d Sir.

I have to advise you of the Death of Mrs. Wager, the Mistress of the Negro School at Williamsburg. I could wish to have revived the Charity, upon such Terms as would be agreeable to you & the rest of the worthy Associates of D.r Bray, but seeing no Prospect of it at present, I have discontinued the School, 'till I can receive your farther Directions. The Acc.t of what I am in Advance you will receive inclosed, Bal.e in my fav.r £11.17.2, for which I have drawn on you in fav.r of Mess.rs Norton & Sons.

Wishing you & the rest of the Associates every Felicity, I remain very respectfully,

Rev.d Sir,

Y.r mo. ob.t Serv.t
Ro. C. Nicholas

Agreed that Thanks be returned to ~~the~~ Rob.t C. N. for that they acquiesce in his Opinion to discontinue ~~the School at present~~ his long Series of Charitable Services, & that he be informed the Associates ~~shall~~ will at any time be very thankful to him for ~~any~~ his Directions how their pious Intentions ~~of the Ass~~ may be most effectually promoted

11

FIVE

Endings and Beginnings, 1774–1777

⁓

Robert Carter Nicholas to Bray Associates, November 17, 1774

Meeting Minutes of the Associates of Dr. Bray, April 1, 1777

On November 17, 1774, Robert Carter Nicholas wrote what appears to have been his final letter to the Associates of Dr. Bray. Ann Wager, the school's teacher, had died three months earlier. In some ways, her death was not a surprise. Already widowed when she accepted the position as the Bray School's live-in teacher, Wager was a subject of regular debate. Trustees often questioned Wager's health and capacity to continue her work in the long term, even though she seemed tireless. Managing thirty or more students ranging from toddlers to near-adolescents seven days a week, she seemed to have been impervious to the physical demands of her work. And yet we know that she was not.

Born around 1716, Ann Wager was nearly fifty years old in 1765 when Robert Carter Nicholas wrote to the Bray Associates about his fears that being the school's sole teacher was becoming too much for her. Already then, Nicholas feared not only for the school's teacher, but for the continuation of the school itself, as noted in his apprehension about replacing Wager should she become infirm or even die. Yet, Wager persevered for almost a decade after Nicholas wrote that letter.

Explaining that Wager's death on August 20, 1774, had necessitated the closure of the Williamsburg Bray School, Nicholas wrote to the Bray Associates, "I have discontinued the School 'till I can receive your farther Directions." The Associates officially consented to this closure in their meeting minutes on March 2, 1775. While anti-British sentiment in the American colonies had not yet reached full-scale revolution, the colonies were questioning their future as part of the British Empire. The First Continental Congress convened in the fall of 1774, and Virginia delegates included Williamsburg's Peyton Randolph, who sent at least three students—Aggy, Roger, and Sam—to the Bray School. It should be noted that Sam later liberated himself in the winter of 1776 by fleeing to join the military forces of Lord Dunmore, the last royal governor of Virginia.

According to the London charity's meeting minutes, the Associates of Dr. Bray had ceased all operations in the British North American colonies by the spring of 1777. The Associates' work would not recommence in North America until 1786, when America emerged from the revolution as a new republic. After 1786, this religious instruction would have a decidedly different tenor than the Bray schools that predated the American Revolution. Regardless, the Associates of Dr. Bray would not resume operations in Williamsburg.

There is much research still to be done on the Associates of Dr. Bray, its schools, and its educative legacy across North America in the eighteenth, nineteenth, and twentieth centuries. What was the enduring impact of the Williamsburg Bray School on its students, and how can that be measured? Former Bray School student Isaac Bee took his leave and attempted to emancipate himself in September 1774 and again in March 1793. Armed with the capacity to read and spell, some former Bray School students, such as Sam, learned of Lord Dunmore's proclamation in November 1775, promising freedom for those who served on the side of the British. Perhaps Bray School students were among those who left New York in 1783 and became part of the Black Loyalist migration to Nova Scotia, Canada, or beyond. The closure of the Williamsburg Bray School in 1774 does not signify an end to the story; it is just the closure of one chapter in the history of Black education in Virginia and the broader African Diaspora.

Letter Transcript
Robert Carter Nicholas to Bray Associates

Virginia 17th Novr 1774

Rev^d. Sir,

    I have to advise you of the Death of M^{rs}. Wager, the Mistress of the Negro School at Williamsburg. I could wish to have revived the Charity upon such Terms as would be agreeable to you & the rest of the worthy Associates of D^r. Bray, but seeing no Prospect of it at present, I have discontinued the School, 'till I can receive your farther Directions. The Acc^t. of what I am in Advance you will receive inclosed, Bal^a. in my fav^r. £11.17.2, for which I have drawn on you in fav^r. of Mess^r. Norton & Sons.

    Wishing & you the rest of the Associates every Felicity, I remain very respectfully,

Rev^d. Sir,
Y^r mo. ob^t. Servt.
Ro. C. Nicholas

Agreed that Thanks be returned to ~~the~~ Robt. C. N. for that they acquiesce in his opinion to discontinue the school at present his long series of Charitable Services & that he be informed ~~th~~ the Associates ~~shall~~ ^{will} at any time ^{be} very thankful to him for ~~any~~ ^{his} Directions how their pious Intentions ~~of the Ass.~~ may be most effectualy promoted

Dr.   The Associates of Doctor Bray   Cr.

1773				1773		
April 1	To Quarter Salary due this day	£5..—..—		Dec.r	By my Exch: to Norton & Son	25..—..—
July 1	To d.o	5..—..—			30 P.Cent	7.10..—
Oct 1	To d.o	5..—..—				32.10..—
					Balance	15. 8. 4
						£ 47.18. 4
1774						
Jan.y 1	To d.o	5..—..—				
April 6	To d.o	5..—..—				
July 2	To d.o	5..—..—				
	To p.d Mr. Blair a Yrs. Rent due 25th Dec.r 1773	10..—..—				
Aug.t 20	To d.o p.d for 7½ Months to the time of Mrs. Wager's death	6. 5..—				
	To p.d Mat: Hatton her Son in Law for Balance of Salary	1.13. 4			By my Exch. to Norton & Son	£ 11.17. 2
		£ 47.18. 4			30 P.Ct	3.11. 1 ½
	To Balance	15. 8. 4				£ 15. 8. 3 ½

E. E. 17th Nov.r 1774
Ro. C. Nicholas

Minutes Transcript
Meeting of the Associates of Dr. Bray

Associates Office 1st April 1777.

Present D^r. Markham   M^r. Pepys
           D^r. Mayo   M^r. S. Waring
           Rev^d. M^r. Waring M^r. Triquet
                                 M^r. Spiller

The pious Designs of the Associates in supporting Negroe School on the Continent of America being at present interrupted by the unhappy Disputes between Great Britain and her Colonies, and there being little Prospect of resuming the same, till an amicable Accommodation shall take place

    Agreed, that in order to answer the pious Intention of our Association it will be adviseable to adopt some other Plan of Charity of a similar Nature, and this Board are of opinion the Establishment and support of Schools in England for the Instruction of poor Children in such Places as shall appear to stand most in need of such charitable Institutions will best correspond with the Interactions of this Society.

Robert Carter Nicholas on the Williamsburg Bray School: An Intersection of Religion and Economy

An essay by Cecilia Weaver

As a trustee of the Williamsburg Bray School, Robert Carter Nicholas was integral to shaping the school's mission and operations. His management of the Bray School's closing, as illustrated in this collection's letters, serves to further highlight this fact. Nicholas was a prominent figure in Williamsburg society, both as a lawyer and treasurer for the colony of Virginia since his appointment to the latter position in 1766. Many written records have been left behind about his life, including frequent advertisements in the *Virginia Gazette* and several published letters featuring his opinions on religious issues. Therefore, analyzing Nicholas's worldview and philosophies can serve to reveal what life may have been like for Bray School students and how the elite of Williamsburg society viewed the institution.

Nicholas's religious views are important to consider within the context of the Bray School's Anglican roots. His influence on religion in Williamsburg extended beyond just that of a private citizen, as he chaired the House of Burgesses' Committee on Religion beginning in 1769. Therefore, Nicholas's public views on religion not only reflect how the Bray School was operated, but also shaped the perspectives of others within the community. The Bray Associates evidently had high regard for Nicholas's religious opinions, as the postscript to the 1774 letter indicates that they would value his advice regarding how best to advance their "pious intentions" after the closing of the Bray School.

These religious opinions include a value placed on uniformity of belief and hierarchy in the established church. Along with Nicholas's involvement in the Bray School, these values are evident in his letter in Purdie and Dixon's June 3, 1773, edition of the *Virginia Gazette*. In his opposition to Samuel Henley's appointment to lead Bruton Parish, Nicholas clearly valued the "uniformity of doctrine" imposed on laypeople by church officials. He argued that ordinary people should not be trusted to form their own opinions about religion, at the risk of "a deplorable condition." Nicholas endorsed a paternalistic view of the church, with only those at the highest level of society permitted to interpret religious texts for others. This aligns with the way one can imagine the Bray School was operated, with a clear delineation of those who were permitted to have an opinion and instruct others, and those who were expected to listen and do what they were told.

Nicholas also viewed the Williamsburg Bray School from an economic perspective. In his letter about closing the school, he devoted a large portion of his writing to the school's accounts and the payment of expenses. This ties into his role as treasurer for the colony of Virginia and the view of enslaved people as part of the economy. In this 1774 letter, Nicholas determined that the most useful statistics for the Bray Associates were centered on the economics of the school: understanding the salaries and debts incurred and how those affected the sum he sent back to England. While he could have included information about progress made in the education of students, he focused purely on the financial aspects of the school. His deference to the Bray Associates in England further reveals a value placed on authority that is similar to his perspective on church hierarchy.

With these views, it is likely that Nicholas supported the Williamsburg Bray School and sent enslaved children there for reasons economic as much as spiritual. The surviving student rosters included Hannah and Sarah, enslaved girls he sent to the Bray School. In the colonial period, enslaved people who could read and perform skilled labor and trades could be of greater value for enslavers. Girls learned to sew at the Bray School, diversifying the types of labor that enslavers could compel these girls to perform.

Clearly, Nicholas's conception of community was in relation to those who had a comparable level of wealth, and he likely viewed enslaved people as little more than a commodity. Nicholas's valuing of authority and his faith in systems further highlight the divide he possibly saw between himself and the Bray School students. The purpose of their education was centered on indoctrination into an existing hierarchical religious and societal structure, rather than the encouragement of free thinking. Thus, the Bray School students were required to adapt to these surroundings and be resilient to use this education for their own purposes, as the goals of the Bray Associates and Robert Carter Nicholas were far from focused on the personal development of the students themselves.

Cecilia Weaver '24 (History, Government) conducted research as an inaugural Student Thought Partner with the William & Mary Bray School Lab, focusing on the Virginia Gazette *Project and an annotated bibliography about the Williamsburg Bray School. She is passionate about creating inclusive historical narratives and plans to pursue a career in public history.*

Personhood in Place of Silence: Reflecting on the Absence of Bray School Scholars in Robert Carter Nicholas's 1774 Letter

An essay by Rachel Hogue

By November 1774, when Robert Carter Nicholas officially informed the Bray Associates of Ann Wager's death that summer, information received by the Associates on the Williamsburg Bray School had been decidedly vague and brief for some time. Due to being "indisposed," Nicholas had for several years before the school's closing failed to send the Associates a crucial piece of information: "a List of the Scholars with proper Remarks on their Progress." In the wake of this administrative lapse, the 1774 Nicholas letter—one of the last definitive records kept by the Bray Associates on the Williamsburg Bray School—is heavy with a particular silence. The glaring absence of the scholars' names and their legal enslaved or free status does not permit us a satisfactory understanding of the Bray School's final student class or the last iteration of its reach across the community.

In the study of the Williamsburg Bray School, students' names hold weight and power. With this power in mind, the absence of scholars' names from the very correspondence that announced the school's closing begs the question of how the children's lives and histories can be illuminated. This is when we can turn to conscientiously imagining the whole lives of the Bray School students, beyond limited and biased archival reference. What we know for certain can be layered with what we cannot know when faced with the silence of the written historical record. Because what is known—what is seen first—is the distinctive absence of the scholars' names. That absence is countered by Nicholas's assessment of Bray School finances and accounts, but his reasons for writing do not tell the entire story.

The numbers meticulously written in Nicholas's final accounting for the school's expenses create a frustrating echo of the way enslaved people were often documented—in the numbered figures of chattel sale rather than in the words of personhood and dignity. What of the personhood and dignity students heard in the names and identities by which their communities knew them, rather than names given by enslavers? When the students walked home from school for the last time, they did not stop learning. They would continue to learn from their kin and community that called them by name with dignity when they came home, when they went to worship, and when they were forced to labor. In the case of the Williamsburg Bray School Scholars, the end of their written presence in these documents does not erase the existence of their personhood. Their histories do not begin and end with their school years or letters sent to the Bray Associates.

At face value, this chapter's letter reads with a sense of finality: the schoolteacher was dead, and the school was closed. When carefully paging through the dozens of Bray Associates archive folders at the Bodleian Libraries in Oxford, England, I read this short letter and the record of its arrival in London to effectively end their administrative connections to Williamsburg. In the wake of the American Revolution, the Bray Associates ceased financial support of schools for Black children in the soon-to-be United States of America. They swiftly moved on to their self-described 'pious intentions,' shifting their focus to schools in England and "Instruction of poor Children in such Places as shall appear to stand most in need of such charitable Institutions."

Although "Williamsburgh" and letters from Robert Carter Nicholas ceased to fill the written record by the late 1770s, the lives of the scholars were far from over in 1774. The students who attended the Williamsburg Bray School cannot be thought of as stalled in childhood. They were not arbitrarily frozen in their schoolhouse just because their teacher's death did not leave local trustees with a clear path forward. They grew up, either enslaved or free, and lived out resistance in every act of individuality, cleverness, and wit they exhibited in the face of enslavers and a larger sociopolitical structure designed to keep them in chattel or quasi-chattel status.

The countless descendants of the Williamsburg Bray School students are the collective proof of a legacy of resilience, and their names and words make up much of the very book you hold—a new archive that is no longer so silent. As you come to the end of this book, go back through the pages, and sit with the names we do have in print, the letters where scholars' names were written down. Read the names we know for certain and imagine the ones we do not.

Rachel Hogue '24 (History) is a graduate of William & Mary. As a member of the first cohort of Student Thought Partners at the William & Mary Bray School Lab, she contributed to the Bray School Records Project, and subsequently conducted research as an intern for The Colonial Williamsburg Foundation. She is humbled to have helped tell the story of the Williamsburg Bray School Scholars.

Closing the Williamsburg Bray School

An essay by Dawn Edmiston

On November 17, 1774, notice was given that the social experiment known as the Williamsburg Bray School had been discontinued. The existing documents from this time are light on words but provide critical perspectives as we attempt to understand the root causes of the school's closure.

As we learned in earlier chapters of this book, continuous challenges plagued the establishment and operation of the Williamsburg Bray School. The very nature of the school's funding from an organization with a mission to spread English literacy and Christianity meant the expected outcomes would be inherently aligned with this mission as well.

On the surface, the two documents related to the school's closing might lead the reader to believe that timing was the fundamental reason for the decision to discontinue operations. The very first statement of the letter from Robert Carter Nicholas to the Bray Associates in 1774 is, "I have to advise you of the Death of Mrs. Wager, the Mistress of the Negro School at Williamsburg." Perhaps continuing the Williamsburg Bray School without the dedicated teacher who had served since its inception was simply too difficult.

However, the remainder of the letter leaves the reader feeling as though Ann Wager's death was not the primary challenge to the sustainability of the Bray School. Nicholas struggled with the Bray Associates to gain additional funding and support for the school, and "seeing no prospect of it at present," he determined that he had no choice but to formally "discontinue" the school. Still, his request for "farther Directions" would seem to infer hope that additional guidance, and perhaps even resources, would be forthcoming.

One is left to wonder about the time preceding this letter, as five years had passed since the last known surviving school report with student list was issued in 1769. What discussions had taken place between 1769 and 1774? And what exactly had the Bray Associates expected the school to achieve during this time? The Bray School was an educational enterprise built around Anglican tenets with a pro-slavery ethos. As a professor of marketing, I am struck by how these children were being educated (or indoctrinated) to become more marketable assets, valued for either their utility, morality, or a combination of both. The Bray schools were, perhaps, the nation's first formal social experiment in the business of Black education: however, the students' actual lived experiences might not have been anticipated or accepted by the Bray Associates.

In addition to being administrator for the Williamsburg Bray School, Nicholas had served as the Virginia colony's treasurer since 1766, so it is not surprising that attached to the end of the 1774 letter is a final accounting of school-related expenses. This focus on finances reminds us of the need to examine the history of the Bray School through a realistic lens rather than a romanticized one. The Bray Associates funded most of the school's expenses, including rent, Wager's salary, and instructional materials such as *The Book of Common Prayer*. Based on the tone of Nicholas's letter, tensions had arisen between the school's perceived needs and the Associates' proposed budget.

Earlier documentation from 1769 suggests that Nicholas was previously met with resistance when he attempted to gain additional funding from the Associates. At that time, the Associates countered that enslavers should be contributing financial resources to the school since the outcome of this initiative would increase the students' value to the enslavers and the community.

What remains unspoken throughout this time is the actual impact of the Bray School on the lives of these enslaved and free Black children. Did the education of these children have the desired effect that the Bray Associates expected when launching the school? Or were students gaining greater confidence in their abilities and becoming increasingly independent in their thinking?

In the end, it seems fortuitous that the Bray School opened in Williamsburg, a colonial city that would be reimagined in the 1920s and reimagined again nearly a hundred years later—when restoring the original building where Ann Wager taught hundreds of Black children. One can only imagine the educational experiences in this building and whether the "lessons learned" are what society expected. Although the Bray Associates decided to discontinue the school, there are undoubtedly many lessons we have yet to learn from this educational enterprise. As one chapter ends, a new chapter begins as the William & Mary Bray School Lab strives to use the Bray School story to help "transform traditional accounts of America's history into a multi-layered story that centers Black legacy at the heart of U.S. democracy."

Dawn Edmiston, DM, EdD, is the clinical professor of marketing at William & Mary. Her first teaching appointment as a visiting faculty member at Howard University inspired her to leave corporate America and pursue a career in higher education. She recently served as a Fulbright Scholar in Estonia and co-authored the book, Marketing Management *(Cognella). Edmiston also served as an Office of Strategic Cultural Partnerships Faculty Fellow.*

Where Have We Been? The Williamsburg Bray School's Closure, Freedom Making, and the Black Educational Tradition

An essay by Jajuan S. Johnson

The Williamsburg Bray School's closure in August 1774 is a critical point of discussion by historians and researchers, in part because of the silence surrounding the school's discontinuation. Its fourteen years of student progress reflected in the previous letters would have warranted the school's continuation. Ann Wager, the school's only teacher, had died, and the schooling of enslaved and free children in Williamsburg abruptly ended with minimal deliberation.

Based on the brutal realities of slavery, one could infer that the rapid judgment to end the school reflected the general devaluation of Black life in eighteenth-century Virginia. Whatever the intent or circumstances, the school was a resource that some enslaved and free Black people used in ways we cannot fully understand. So, how did enslaved and free Black people respond to the dilemma of the school closing on the cusp of the Revolutionary War? This reflective essay encourages readers to consider that the Williamsburg Bray School existed in the context of Black people who understood the value of education as a path to freedom and a means of survival in a slave society.

In Heather Andrea Williams's *Self-Taught: African American Education in Slavery and Freedom*, the central research question is, "What did ordinary African Americans in the South do to provide education for themselves during slavery and when slavery ended?" Centralizing archives curated by African Americans such as slave narratives, autobiographies, oral histories, and Freedmen's Bureau records, Williams offers a rendering of Black education during slavery and afterward. She provides a history of Black people finding creative and subversive ways to learn while legally prohibited. Williams chronicles how African Americans built schools after the Civil War and later advocated for education as a civil right that transformed education in the South for Black and non-Black people. Williams's research is a genealogy of the African American dedication to education, which is essential when contextualizing the Williamsburg Bray School. In as much as the school was used to subjugate Black children, some understood that the power of becoming literate in any context could break slavery's chains.

Although finding eighteenth-century primary sources on African Americans in Williamsburg has its challenges, we learn how Black people valued education through the free people who sent their children to the Williamsburg Bray School. Numerous scholars and genealogists record that John Insco Bee, the father of Isaac, Johanna, and Clara Bee, was a free man who ensured that his children became literate at the school. Also, Matthew Ashby, the father of Harry, John, and Mary Ashby saw the importance of the school and enrolled his children. As we read between the lines of the extant texts, we may find clues about the lives of the children and how they likely used the instruction obtained from the school. The testimonies of their descendants can provide insight into their liberatory use of education.

The Williamsburg Bray School's history and physical presence were relatively obscure until the re-discovery of the original eighteenth-century structure in 2020. The school was not etched in the collective memory of local Black communities in ways that the later James City County Training School, Bruton Heights School, and Oak Grove School were. These sites of racial uplift were produced by Black citizens who challenged and upended inequities enshrined in United States law and cultural practice. Also, these schools grew out of earlier Black schools in the Williamsburg area as noted in "LIFE IN VIRGINIA By a Yankee Teacher," written by post-Civil War missionary educator

Margaret Newbold Thorpe. She taught newly freed children and adults at Fort Magruder and in Williamsburg, noting the rapid speed of student learning and documenting that older adults who attended at night traveled six miles to learn. Thorpe's diary suggests an already intact Black educational tradition spurred the yearning for knowledge that even slavery could not obliterate.

So, where is the Williamsburg Bray School situated in the history of Black education in Virginia's Historic Triangle? It exists in the sphere of African American knowledge-making in late-eighteenth-century Williamsburg. The school is not a singular feature in eighteenth-century African American education in Williamsburg. Also, in as much as there was learning at the school, it is worth considering that based on the religious miseducation that reinforced Black subjugation, it is plausible that "unlearning" occurred within enslaved communities, as some interpreted literacy as a pathway to freedom. So, perhaps the closure of the Williamsburg Bray School was partly a new beginning for some enslaved and free children who had enhanced their repertoire of intellectual tools for freedom and survival.

Jajuan S. Johnson, PhD, served as the Mellon Postdoctoral Fellow for The Lemon Project at William & Mary, and is now Public Historian for Research Programs, William & Mary Libraries and The Lemon Project. As a public historian and heritage studies scholar, his research explores the power of places of difficult histories to cultivate public emotion and generate a collective sense of community in the aftermath of traumatizing events of the distant and recent pasts.

A Legacy of Learning:
Archaeology at the Williamsburg Bray School

An essay by Ashley McCuistion

As the Williamsburg Bray School closed its doors in August of 1774, a new chapter of American history was beginning. A nation was forming, and every resident had a part to play in its development, including the widespread population of enslaved individuals who lived and worked across the colonies. As many as 400 enslaved and free Black children may have passed through the doors of the Williamsburg Bray School during its fourteen years of operation, and the impact of this education is clear in the rapidly rising English literacy rates among enslaved Virginians after 1760. This increase likely reflects not only the influence of the school, but also the impact of the children who brought their lessons home and shared them among friends and family.

Archaeological excavations at the original site of the Williamsburg Bray School have provided valuable insight into students' daily lives during the school's first five years of operation. Over the course of four summers, more than 200,000 artifacts have been recovered from the site, and the discovery of structures like a property fence and privy—or outhouse—have played a vital role in understanding and interpreting the landscape that would have surrounded the school building. These findings paint a complex portrait of a time and place where opportunity, intellect, creativity, and resistance coincided with extreme oppression, racism, and exploitation.

Among the thousands of artifacts recovered from the Bray

School site, there are a handful of objects that tell a particularly compelling story. Fragments of more than twenty slate pencils offer some insight into the school's curriculum, which various accounts suggest included writing, a subject that was highly controversial among eighteenth-century enslavers. Some seventy clay marbles have also been recovered from the site, once scattered across the lawn behind the school building before being buried by more than two centuries of plowing and construction. Most of these marbles are handmade, undecorated, and imperfectly shaped, and the broad range of sizes and colors makes each one unique.

While tying clay marbles to a specific timeframe is difficult, the fact that there are more of them at this site than any residential site excavated in Colonial Williamsburg suggests they are related to the school period. As archaeologists continue to analyze these objects, they hope to determine whether the clay used to make the marbles came from local sources and whether it shares characteristics with local bricks or earthenware pottery. If we can narrow down where the marbles were manufactured, we may be able to determine if the students were making them themselves, if they were coming from local potters or brickyards, or if they were imported from elsewhere.

There are several ways students at the Bray School could have been using marbles, from learning to count to playing games in between lessons. Regardless of their intended function, it is likely the students used them for both purposes, and their widespread presence at the site suggests a snapshot of learning, play, and agency among the students at the school.

In addition to recovered objects like pencils and marbles, there are dozens of different types of ceramic vessels dating to the mid- to late-eighteenth century. The most interesting assemblage came from a two-seated privy located in the yard just behind the Bray School building. Nearly twenty different types of pottery were recovered from the two privy pits, which evidence suggests were filled in around the time the school's operations relocated from Prince George Street to a second site near Custis Square on Francis Street. The vessels recovered from the privy pits represent a broad range of styles and qualities. Many were finely potted table wares imported from Europe, while others were locally made coarse earthenware vessels used for food storage. Found in and around the privy were hundreds of fragments of colonoware vessels—a type of low-fired ceramic made from locally sourced materials that is frequently associated with African American communities in colonial Virginia. The variety of ceramics found in the privy provides some insight into the division of class within the school building and challenges our perception of what makes an object "school related."

While research into the archaeological data recovered from the original Bray School site continues, the objects left behind have already made a tremendous impact on our understanding of the school and of the lives of free and enslaved Black children in colonial Williamsburg. For far too long, the lives, identities, and voices of children—especially those who were enslaved—have remained silent and hidden in the archaeological and historic records. Through projects like these, we can finally illuminate and commemorate the experiences of enslaved children in colonial America, and start to better understand and appreciate how their upbringing and education ultimately shaped them into the adults who would shape American history.

Ashley McCuistion is a staff archaeologist for The Colonial Williamsburg Foundation. She holds degrees in anthropology and archaeology from Virginia Commonwealth University and Indiana University of Pennsylvania, and specializes in historical archaeology and education. She has been directing excavations and managing archaeological analyses and interpretation at the original site of the Williamsburg Bray School since 2022.

Afterword

By Ann Marie Stock

Even before the identity of the Williamsburg Bray School was ascertained, there was hope. Hope for confirming a scholarly hypothesis. Hope for advancing archaeological research and architectural preservation. Hope for shaping family and community histories. Hope for exploring the evolution of education in our country.

As a participant from the very beginning in helping create the Williamsburg Bray School Initiative and bring into being the William & Mary Bray School Lab, I am humbled by the opportunities I have had to connect with extraordinary individuals—each of whom has helped map the trajectory of the Williamsburg Bray School: the descendant who offered her love of vanilla-infused baking as an entree to conversations about race relations; the longtime Williamsburg resident who arrived with a timeworn binder of family letters and photos in hopes of helping advance the research; the couple who painstakingly transcribed hundreds of documents to make information more widely accessible; the social justice advocate who organized an extemporaneous drum circle to invite risk-taking in the company of others; the public school teachers who have activated the Bray School for dance choreography and performance, history and social studies projects, and creative writing and art contributions; and so many others. The Bray School has brought us together, fostering new relationships and strengthening existing ones.

One exceedingly memorable moment was when we came

together to witness the move of the Bray-Digges House, through the streets of Williamsburg, under overhanging branches, from its site on the William & Mary campus to its new home in Colonial Williamsburg's Historic Area. It was exhilarating to live this experience and to do so in the company of so many—descendants of the Bray School students and the Digges family who felt a personal connection; the two hard-hatted presidents, Katherine Rowe and Cliff Fleet, who from the very beginning envisioned the Bray School's potential and understood the importance of joining forces; the investors whose generosity propelled the project forward; colleagues from across the university and the foundation who contributed ideas and lent expertise; students of all ages and their teachers and professors; Tribal leaders from across Virginia; elected officials from the city and the commonwealth; and neighbors and friends. That event was then, and remains now, a turning point for our community.

In a similar vein, this volume mirrors the Williamsburg Bray School Initiative in that it seeks to illuminate and serves as tangible evidence of what is possible when people come together in service of something larger than themselves. It has convened a range of visions and a diversity of voices: descendants, scholars, teachers, students, museum professionals, community activists, genealogists, and others who co-exist in these pages. Guided by their committed and capable co-editors, the contributors examined centuries-old documents, formulated their reflections, and refined their prose. These essays permit us to glimpse the varied ways we make sense of our world by integrating the past with the present to envision a future that is more just and equitable. These original writings augment materials in traditional archives with memory and lived experience to expand our knowledge and enhance understanding, surfacing gaps and partial truths to invite—and indeed insist on—mutual respect, reconciliation, and ongoing exploration.

This volume has proffered a model for "doing" history. Like the Williamsburg Bray School Initiative, it has invited us in, empowered us to experience the pleasure and privilege of coming together—and the responsibility of being part of this ongoing endeavor. While there is still much to learn—about the school, the students, their descendants, and their roles in shaping this country—what we do know is that the Bray School is already making a difference. From our significant locale in the Commonwealth of Virginia, at this crucial moment as we anticipate the 250th anniversary of the signing of the Declaration of Independence, we are contributing to a more comprehensive and nuanced understanding of our nation's past and its potential for the future. We are crafting—with candor and rigor, and with respect for our collaborators—effective ways to facilitate dialogues across difference, ensure equity, and expand understanding. We are honored to be serving as a model for others who seek our guidance and insight as they, too, undertake this important and daunting work.

Perhaps the loftiest hope of all—that of coming together—is evidenced by our efforts to ensure that "the structure and the stories"—the building and the discoveries—concerning the Williamsburg Bray School have the greatest possible impact. Together William & Mary and The Colonial Williamsburg Foundation have raised funds to restore and relocate the structure and conduct research, consulted with descendant and other community members to make decisions and develop programming, connected university students and faculty with museum professionals, and created curricula and learning opportunities for K-12 teachers and students. Together we have shared our findings in our community, across the nation, and, increasingly, around the world.

The Williamsburg Bray School is providing the "common ground" on which we can continue to create community in our region and far beyond, and thereby strengthen our democracy. This certainly does inspire hope.

Ann Marie Stock, PhD, is Presidential Liaison for Strategic Cultural Partnerships and Chancellor Professor of Modern Languages at William & Mary.

Linking the Present with the Past

A Genealogy Supplement by Elizabeth Drembus

While the Williamsburg Bray School building is undergoing restoration and preservation by The Colonial Williamsburg Foundation, the William & Mary Bray School Lab is likewise engaged in a restoration effort through genealogical research. We are reconstructing the family lines of the Bray School Scholars—the boys and girls who attended the school. The goal of the project is to reconnect the Descendant Community, here in the Williamsburg area and beyond, to the history and legacy of the Williamsburg Bray School.

Genealogists are always looking for connections. In this case, with the surviving attendance lists for 1762, 1765, and 1769, we follow clues left behind by children who played, laughed, labored, worshipped, and made their way in the world connected to their families and their communities. The lists raise so many questions and we strive to learn all that we can about the scholars. Through the research, we are restoring those familial and community ties while also discovering new connections. To be successful, the project relies equally on the three elements of engaging the Descendant Community, researching the records, and sharing the stories.

ENGAGING THE DESCENDANT COMMUNITY

The collective knowledge held by the members of the Bray School Descendant Community is vital to this work. Their willingness to partner with us brings a perspective to the research that cannot be found merely in dusty, old documents. By meeting with the

Descendant Community and listening to their guidance, a more complete picture is uncovered as they share oral histories and knowledge about names, places, and local history. The African American community with continuous roots in the Williamsburg area is speaking and is heard in this project.

RESEARCHING THE RECORDS

Traditional genealogy begins with the present and moves to the past through documents such as vital records, newspapers, census records, wills, and deeds. The genealogical research for the Bray School Scholars is following that same path as we work with the Descendant Community members and study family records in the search for their ancestors. We are also conducting reverse genealogy, starting in the colonial era with the names of the scholars and moving forward in time through the records. We find their names in wills, estate inventories, tax records, and chancery court records.

SHARING THE STORIES

The Bray School letters do not tell us how the children felt, who their friends were, or what they imagined. Large parts of their stories have been lost. What the records are revealing, however, is the truth of slavery's legacy. So far, the records show how the scholars' families were often fractured. There is the story of Aggy (1765) and her children—Kitty, Betsey, and Nathan. After the death of Peyton and Betty Randolph, Aggy (with Betsey and Nathan) had to leave Williamsburg, and travel to the household of Benjamin Harrison at Berkeley in nearby Charles City County. Kitty's story continued in chancery court records. Kitty and her children were sent with Elizabeth Harrison, eventually living at Stoneland, Lewis Burwell's plantation in Mecklenburg County, Virginia. Another story of separation involves Molly (1765), who was enslaved in the William Prentis household. Molly and her five siblings (Effy, Jemmy, Pompey, Nancy, and Tom) and their mother, Judith, were divided between several Prentis heirs after the deaths of William Prentis; his wife, Mary; and his daughter, Elizabeth.

And yet, we also get glimpses of the scholars' resilience and determination that their legacies would be carried forward. We see evidence in family naming patterns as names are passed down from one generation to the next, such as Kitty naming her son Nathan for her brother. The records also reveal parents' hopes for their children. In his will, Matthew Ashby provided for the continued education of his children, John and Mary. This legacy of education's importance continues to be passed down through Ashby descendants today.

FINDING AND FOLLOWING THEIR FOOTSTEPS

Much like uncovering the original floorboards of the Williamsburg Bray School during the restoration and preservation phase, the genealogical research also uncovers what has been hidden and marginalized. When we see the wear patterns on the floorboards of the restored building, we are reminded that what we read are not simply names on lists. We recognize the humanity of the Bray School Scholars. It is hard, painstakingly slow work. However, the restoration of the scholars' stories and of family connections is necessary work. Voices seek to be heard—voices of Descendant Community members and voices of the children and their family members whose stories we have the privilege and responsibility to tell. Each time a record reveals a name, that person calls out to us from the past. "Here I am. I lived, breathed, and had a life. Tell my story."

Elizabeth Drembus is the genealogist for the William & Mary Bray School Lab, Office of Strategic Cultural Partnerships. Prior to joining William & Mary, she was a genealogist with the National Society Daughters of the American Revolution (DAR) and a member of the research team for the Virginia Theological Seminary's Reparations Research Project. Drembus is leading the efforts to identify and document the genealogical lines of all known Williamsburg Bray School students from the eighteenth through the twenty-first centuries.

Acknowledgments

Seeing this book come together is the realization of a dream that began almost immediately after the William & Mary Bray School Lab was launched publicly in October 2021. We envisioned a project like this, but we could never have imagined how well it would come together or how much support it would receive so quickly.

We would like to thank everyone we work with under the umbrella of the Williamsburg Bray School Initiative, the innovative partnership between William & Mary and The Colonial Williamsburg Foundation. We extend our deepest gratitude, especially, to President Katherine Rowe, President Cliff Fleet, and Presidential Liaison Ann Marie Stock. We would also like to thank Carrie Cooper, Lisa Nickel, and staff at William & Mary Libraries for their support.

Catherine Whittenburg, Jody Macenka, and Katie Roy are our Colonial Williamsburg Foundation editorial and publishing partners. Thank you for believing in this dream from the beginning, and for moving mountains to make this a reality. It has been an honor to collaborate with you.

The William & Mary Bray School Lab acknowledges the support of donors, public and private, named and anonymous, including the Commonwealth of Virginia, Steve and Gale Kohlhagen, the Mellon Foundation, the Jessie Ball duPont Fund, the Ametek Foundation, and the Middle Plantation Foundation. Your partnerships have ensured our ability to advance the mission of studying, preserving, and sharing broadly the history and legacies of the Williamsburg Bray School and its young scholars.

We wish to extend our deepest gratitude to our early cohort of

ACKNOWLEDGMENTS

Student Thought Partners who worked tirelessly transcribing and otherwise poring over the letters included in this book: Madeline Dort, Rachel Hogue, Emily Knoeppel, Ye Xiao, Mary Hannah Grier, Cecilia Weaver, and Olivia Blackshire. However, we extend continued appreciation to *all* our Student Thought Partners, past and present, for the dedication and professionalism they exhibit in the William & Mary Bray School Lab every day. Highest professional thanks to collection specialists at the United Society for the Propagation of the Gospel (USPG), the University of Oxford, and the University of Virginia for sharing the records that are central to this project.

Most importantly, we owe a debt of gratitude to all our contributors—especially members of the Williamsburg Bray School Descendant Community. We thank you for your willingness to engage with these difficult subjects and create a dynamic collection of essays we now share with a world made better by your work.

Maureen Elgersman Lee
Nicole Brown

Bibliography / For Further Reading

WILLIAMSBURG BRAY SCHOOL WEBSITES

William & Mary Bray School Lab: https://www.wm.edu/sites/brayschool/

A Reasonable Progress: The Blog of the W&M Bray School Lab: https://brayschool.pages.wm.edu/

Colonial Williamsburg: https://colonialwilliamsburg.org/bray

ARCHIVES

Margaret Newbold Thorpe. "LIFE IN VIRGINIA By a Yankee Teacher" and "Life in North Carolina." William & Mary Libraries, Special Collections Research Center, 1951.

Minutes of the Meetings of the 'Associates of Dr. Bray', 1729-1735. In the Papers of the Society for the Propagation of the Gospel in Foreign Parts, Bray Associates Collection (1699-1979), F1a. Weston Library, University of Oxford, Oxford, UK.

Minutes of the Meetings of the 'Associates of Dr. Bray', 1736-1768. In the Papers of the Society for the Propagation of the Gospel in Foreign Parts, Bray Associates Collection (1699-1979), F2a. Weston Library, University of Oxford, Oxford, UK.

William Hunter, Robert Carter Nicholas, and Managers of Williamsburg Negro School Correspondence from Virginia to Bray Associates, 1761-1774. In the Papers of the Society for the Propagation of the Gospel in Foreign Parts, Bray

BIBLIOGRAPHY / FOR FURTHER READING

Associates Collection (1699-1979), North America Files, Vol. 1, F2. Weston Library, University of Oxford, Oxford, UK.

Thomas Jefferson and Jefferson-Randolph Family Papers, 1747-1827. In the Tracy W. McGregor Library of American History, Accession #564, 6746, Albert H. and Shirley Small Special Collections Library, University of Virginia, Charlottesville, VA.

BOOKS

Belvin, Ed. *Williamsburg Facts & Fiction 1900-1950*. Williamsburg: Printwell, 2002.

Berry, Diana Ramey. *The Price for Their Pound of Flesh: The Value of the Enslaved, from Womb to Grave, in the Building of a Nation*. Reprint edition. Boston: Beacon Press, 2017.

DeJulio, Samuel, and Leah Durán, eds. *Exploring and Expanding Literacy Histories of the United States: A Spotlight on Under-Recognized Histories*. Boca Raton: Routledge, 2024.

DuBois, W. E. B. *The Souls of Black Folk*, 1903. Various editions.

Gallay, Alan. *Indian Slavery in Colonial America*. Lincoln: University of Nebraska Press, 2009.

Gerbner, Katharine. *Christian Slavery: Conversion and Race in the Protestant Atlantic World*. Early American Studies. Philadelphia: University of Pennsylvania Press, 2018.

Glasson, Travis. *Mastering Christianity: Missionary Anglicanism and Slavery in the Atlantic World*. New York: Oxford University Press, 2012.

Hartman, Saidiya V. *Scenes of Subjection: Terror, Slavery, and Self-Making in Nineteenth-Century America*. New York: Oxford University Press, 1997.

Hughes, Langston. *The Dream Keeper and Other Poems*. New York: Knopf Books for Young Readers, 1996.

Maccubbin, Robert P., ed. *Williamsburg, Virginia: A City Before the State 1699-1999*. Williamsburg: City of Williamsburg, 2000.

Moretti-Langholtz, Danielle, Buck Woodard, et. al. *Building the Brafferton: The Founding, Funding, and Legacy of America's Indian School*. Williamsburg: Muscarelle Museum of Art, 2019.

Shinn, Florence Scovel. *Your Word Is Your Wand*. Wilder Publications, 2009.

Trouillot, Michel-Rolph. *Silencing the Past: Power and the Production of History*. Boston: Beacon Press, 1995.

Williams, Heather Andrea. *Self-Taught: African American Education in Slavery and Freedom*. Chapel Hill: University of North Carolina Press, 2007.

Woodson, Carter G. *The Education of the Negro Prior to 1861: A History of the Education of the Colored People of the United States from the Beginning of Slavery to the Civil War*. Washington, D.C, 1915.

BRAY SCHOOL TEXTBOOKS*

Bacon, Rev. Thomas. *Two Sermons, Preached to a Congregation of Black Slaves, at the Parish Church of S.P. in the Province of Maryland. By an American Pastor*. London: J. Oliver, 1749.

Bacon, Rev. Thomas. *Four Sermons: Upon the Great and Indispensable Duty of All Christian Masters and Mistresses to Bring Up Their Negro Slaves in the Knowledge and Fear of God. Preached at the Parish Church of St Peter in Talbot County, in the Province of Maryland*. London: J. Oliver, 1750.

The Child's First Book, 1774. http://digital.francke-halle.de/fsaad/1270571.

Dixon, Thomas. *The English instructor or, the art of spelling improved. Being a more Plain, Easy, and Regular Method of Teaching Young Children, than any extant. In two parts...* London: C. Hitch, S. Crowder, et. al., 1760. 23rd edition.

Thomas, Lord Bishop of Sodor and Man. *An Essay Towards An Instruction For The Indians; Explaining the most Essential Doctrines of Christianity*. London: J. Osborn and W. Thorn, 1740.

---

*It should be noted that there are considerably more textbooks than the ones listed above which were sent to the Williamsburg Bray School. For a list of every Williamsburg Bray School textbook sent in 1760, please refer to this transcription:https://digital.libraries.wm.edu/reverend-john-waring-reverend-thomas-dawson-february-29-1760

BIBLIOGRAPHY / FOR FURTHER READING

"[Rev. John Waring] A Letter to an American Planter from His Friend in London, 10 October 1770." In *Religious Philanthropy and Colonial Slavery: The American Correspondence of the Associates of Dr. Bray, 1717-1777*, edited by John C. Van Horne, 293–302. Urbana: University of Illinois Press, 1985.

DESCENDANT MONOGRAPHS AND COMMUNITY RESOURCES

Ashby, William M. *Tales Without Hate*. 2nd edition. USA: Upland Press, 1996.

Bridgeforth-Williams, Jacqueline. "The Village: The Initiative for Equity in Education." The Village (WJCC). https://www.villagewjcc.org/

"Engaging Descendant Communities in the Interpretation of Slavery at Museums and Historic Sites." The National Summit on Teaching Slavery: National Trust for Historic Preservation & James Madison's Montpelier, African American Cultural Heritage Action Fund, 2018.

Jones, Col. Lafayette, Jr. *My Great, Great, Grandfather's Journey to An Island of Freedom in The Middle of Slavery*. Williamsburg: Jenlaf Publishing, 2008.

DIGITAL RESOURCES

"A course of lectures upon the church catechism in four volumes. Vol. I. Upon the preliminary questions and answers by a divine of the Church of England." In the digital collection *Early English Books Online 2*. University of Michigan Library Digital Collections. https://name.umdl.umich.edu/A29256.0001.001.

Bly, Antonio T. "Slave Literacy and Education in Virginia." *Encyclopedia Virginia*, June 24, 2019. https://www.encyclopediavirginia.org/Slave_Literacy_and_Education_in_Virginia#start_entry.

'Bray Schools' in Canada, America and the Bahamas, 1645-1900. British Online Archives, https://microform.digital/boa/

collections/30/bray-schools-in-canada-america-and-the-bahamas-1645-1900.

Chhaya, Priya. "Stories & Structure: The History of Black Education at the Williamsburg Bray School." National Trust for Historic Preservation, October 12, 2022. https://savingplaces.org/stories/stories-and-structure-the-history-of-black-education-at-the-williamsburg-bray-school.

The Colonial Williamsburg Foundation, Aaron Lovejoy, and Nicole Brown. "Williamsburg Bray School Map." The Colonial Williamsburg Foundation, February 3, 2023. https://www.colonialwilliamsburg.org/learn/research-and-education/architectural-research/williamsburg-bray-school-initiative/williamsburg-bray-school-map/.

Covart, Liz. "Discovery of the Williamsburg Bray School." *Ben Franklin's World*, August 11, 2022. https://benfranklinsworld.com/episode-331-discovery-of-the-williamsburg-bray-school/.

Kelly, Mary Louise. "Discovery Of Schoolhouse for Black Children Now Offers a History Lesson." *All Things Considered*. NPR, March 6, 2021. https://www.npr.org/2021/03/03/973355524/discovery-of-schoolhouse-for-black-children-now-offers-a-history-lesson.

Miller, Patricia. "History on the Move." *Encyclopedia Virginia*, April 10, 2023. https://encyclopediavirginia.org/history-on-the-move/.

Starecheski, Laura. "Take The ACE Quiz — And Learn What It Does and Doesn't Mean." *NPR*, March 2, 2015, sec. What Shapes Health. https://www.npr.org/sections/health-shots/2015/03/02/387007941/take-the-ace-quiz-and-learn-what-it-does-and-doesnt-mean.

Wolfe, Brendan. "The Associates of Dr. Bray and the Bray Schools." *Encyclopedia Virginia*, December 7, 2020. https://encyclopediavirginia.org/entries/associates-of-dr-bray/.

EDITED VOLUMES

Van Horne, John C., ed. *Religious Philanthropy and Colonial Slavery: The American Correspondence of the Associates of Dr. Bray, 1717-1777*. Urbana: University of Illinois Press, 1985.

BIBLIOGRAPHY / FOR FURTHER READING

JOURNAL ARTICLES

Anesko, Michael. "So Discreet a Zeal: Slavery and the Anglican Church in Virginia, 1680-1730." *The Virginia Magazine of History and Biography* 93, no. 3 (July 1985): 247–78.

Betti, Colleen. "'They Gave the Children China Dolls': Toys, Socialization, and Gendered Labor on American Plantations." *Journal of African Diaspora Archaeology and Heritage* 11, no. 2 (May 2022): 97–129.

Bly, Antonio T. "'Pretends he can read': Runaways and Literacy in Colonial America, 1730-1776." *Early American Studies* 6, no. 2 (Fall 2008): 261–94.

Bly, Antonio T. "In Pursuit of Letters: A History of the Bray Schools for Enslaved Children in Colonial Virginia." *History of Education Quarterly* 51, no. 4 (November 2011): 429–59.

Bly, Antonio T. "'Reed through the Bybell': Slave Education in Early Virginia." *Book History* 16 (2013): 1–33.

Meyers, Terry L. "A First Look at the Worst: Slavery and Race Relations at the College of William and Mary. *William and Mary Bill of Rights Journal* 16, no. 4 (April 2008): 1141-1168.

Meyers, Terry L. "Benjamin Franklin, the College of William and Mary, and the Williamsburg Bray School." *Anglican and Episcopal History* 79, no. 4 (December 2010): 368–93.

Meyers, Terry L. "Thinking About Slavery at the College of William and Mary." *William and Mary Bill of Rights Journal* 21, no. 4 (May 2013): 1215-1256.

Pennington, Edgar Legare. "Thomas Bray's Associates and Their Work Among the Negroes." *American Antiquarian Society* 48, no. 2 (October 1938): 311–403.

Shelling, Richard I. "Benjamin Franklin and the Dr. Bray Associates." *Pennsylvania Magazine of History and Biography* 63, no. 3 (July 1939): 282–93.

Stanton, Grant E. and John C. Van Horne. "The Philadelphia Bray Schools: A Story of Black Education in Early America, 1758–1845." *The Pennsylvania Magazine of History and Biography* 147, no. 3 (October 2023): 75-104.

NEWSPAPER AND MAGAZINE ARTICLES

Aron, Paul. "Learning about the School: Research is Challenging the Assumptions about the Building that Housed the Bray School." *Trend & Tradition–The Magazine of Colonial Williamsburg*, Summer 2022.

Cramer, Maria. "University Finds 18th-Century Schoolhouse Where Black Children Learned to Read." *The New York Times*, February 26, 2021.

Davis-Marks, Isis. "University Building Identified as One of the U.S.' First Schools for Black Children." Smart News. *Smithsonian Magazine*, March 3, 2021.

Elgersman Lee, Maureen. "The World of the Williamsburg Bray School: A School for Enslaved and Free Black Children Was Established at a Time of Profound Changes Worldwide." *Trend & Tradition–The Magazine of Colonial Williamsburg*, Spring 2022.

Heim, Joe. "At William & Mary, a School for Free and Enslaved Black Children is Rediscovered." *The Washington Post*, February 25, 2021, sec. Education.

Trifone, Nicole. "On a Mission: Ann Wager's Purpose in Teaching Free and Enslaved Black Students Was Grounded in Religion." *Trend & Tradition–The Magazine of Colonial Williamsburg*, Autumn 2018.

RESEARCH DATABASES

William & Mary Bray School Lab Digital Research Database. William & Mary Libraries Digital Collections, William & Mary, Williamsburg, VA. https://digital.libraries.wm.edu/node/92737.

RESEARCH REPORTS

Brown, Nicole. "Preliminary Williamsburg Bray School Historical Research Report, Block 14 Building 41." Williamsburg: The Colonial Williamsburg Foundation Publications, 2024. https://cwfpublications.omeka.net/items/show/2657.

BIBLIOGRAPHY / FOR FURTHER READING

The Colonial Williamsburg Foundation and Scholars. "Enslaving Virginia." Williamsburg: The Colonial Williamsburg Foundation Publications, 1998. https://cwfpublications.omeka.net/items/show/170.

Rowe, Linda H. *A History of Black Education and Bruton Heights School, Williamsburg, Virginia.* Research Report Series-0373. Williamsburg: The Colonial Williamsburg Foundation Publications, 1997. https://research.colonialwilliamsburg.org/DigitalLibrary/view/index.cfm?doc=ResearchReports%5CRR0373.xml.

Stephenson, Mary A. "Notes on the Negro School in Williamsburg, 1760-1774." Research Report Series-0126. Williamsburg: The Colonial Williamsburg Foundation Publications, 1963. https://research.colonialwilliamsburg.org/DigitalLibrary/view/index.cfm?doc=ResearchReports%5CRR0126.xml.

Tate, Thad W., Jr. "The Negro in Eighteenth-Century Williamsburg." Research Report Series-0121. Williamsburg: The Colonial Williamsburg Foundation Publications, 1957. https://research.colonialwilliamsburg.org/DigitalLibrary/view/index.cfm?doc=ResearchReports%5CRR0121.xml.

About the Editors

Maureen Elgersman Lee, DA, is director of the William & Mary Bray School Lab and the former Mellon Engagement Coordinator for African American Heritage, Office of Strategic Cultural Partnerships. A professor of African American history for more than two decades, Elgersman Lee has held faculty positions in universities in Georgia, Maine, and Virginia, and is a former director of the Black History Museum and Cultural Center of Virginia. An award-winning author, she has published widely on the history of people of African descent in Canada, the United States, and the British Caribbean. She could not do what she does without the enduring encouragement and support of her husband and daughters.

Nicole Brown is graduate assistant for the William & Mary Bray School Lab, Office of Strategic Cultural Partnerships, and a PhD candidate in American Studies at William & Mary. Brown is also a former program design manager at The Colonial Williamsburg Foundation as well as a public historian who portrays Ann Wager, the white teacher at the Williamsburg Bray School. Her ongoing research centers Black literacy in the Atlantic World via interdisciplinary and descendant-engaged scholarship. She would like to thank her wonderful husband, parents, and extended family for always encouraging her to use her voice in service of speaking truth.